FIVE EXPERIMENTAL COLLEGES

Bensalem

Antioch-Putney

Franconia

Old Westbury

Fairhaven

Edited by

GARY B. MACDONALD

Harper & Row, Publishers

New York • Evanston • San Francisco • London

Grateful acknowledgement is made for permission to reprint the following:

"Start with People," first published in *Fordham* magazine. Copyright © 1967 by Elizabeth Sewell. Reprinted by permission of the author and of the editor of *Fordham.*

Excerpts from "The Fireflies and the Bull: An Anatomy of Bullshit," by Roy P. Fairfield, *The Humanist,* March/April 1970. Reprinted by permission.

"Lies" by Yevgeny Yevtushenko from *Yevtushenko: Selected Poems.* Copyright © 1962 by Robin Milner-Gulland and Peter Levi. Reprinted by permission of E.P. Dutton.

Lines from "The Conflict" by C. Day-Lewis. Reprinted by permission of Harold Matson Co., Inc.

Excerpts from *Mr. Sammler's Planet* by Saul Bellow. Copyright © 1969, 1970 by Saul Bellow. All rights reserved. Reprinted by permission of the Viking Press, Inc.

Lines from "Little Gidding," from *Four quartets* by T. S. Eliot. Copyright © 1943 by T. S. Eliot, renewed 1971 by Esme Valery Eliot. Reprinted by permission of Harcourt Brace Jovanovich, Inc.

FIVE EXPERIMENTAL COLLEGES

LIBRARY OF CONGRESS CATALOG CARD NUMBER: 72–85780

STANDARD BOOK NUMBER: 06–136109–7

Designed by Yvette A. Vogel

for Star Route,
its peace and the people who live there

Acknowledgements

For invaluable support and assistance in editing this book, I owe a great debt of gratitude to Donald McLeod, Frank James, Ray, Pat, Sharon and Harvey at Fairhaven College; Dick and Allison, friends extraordinaire, and, of course, Elizabeth Sewell. Also, a long-standing debt of thanks for encouragement is due Annis Hovde, one of those rare professors who is also a friend.

CONTENTS

II. ANTIOCH-PUTNEY
GRADUATE SCHOOL
OF EDUCATION

Contents vii

Realities:
Growth by Fire

For the last, touching impossibility, I take it those things are to be held possible which may be done by some person, though not by everyone; and which may be done by many, though not by any one; and which may be done in succession of ages, though not within the hour-glass of one man's life. . . .

FRANCIS BACON
The Advancement of Learning

Introduction

This is a book about educational change. Indirectly, the essays that follow may foreshadow what could happen when change occurs in a huge, systematized institution which is nevertheless important to the survival of better aspects of American culture. The institution is American higher education. The change is the creation of experimental colleges within that system. Directly, and from experience, this book deals with what this change actually has meant to five particular experimental colleges, primarily during the last decade. Indeed, the colleges themselves were sources and heralds of educational change. Their stories form a subjective "psychologue" about the dangers and joys of rapid, careful, if not always careful enough, innovation inside the higher learning Establishment in the United States today.

We concern ourselves here with Antioch-Putney Graduate School of Education, headquartered in Putney, Vermont; Bensalem College, a division of Fordham University in the Bronx; Fairhaven College, a division of Western Washington State College in Bellingham; Franconia College, in Franconia Village, New Hampshire; and the State University of New York College at Old Westbury, located on Long Island. Many more experimental colleges and programs exist about which we have not spoken. By the same token, there has not been any painstaking selection of "representative" places from among the many more than one hundred experimental programs now enrolling students in the United States. We have not considered, for example, the "free universities" springing up everywhere or the several innovative pilot blocs of courses and majors and minors now being tested on many American campuses. Rather, we have taken what friendship and chance have given us. We have compiled a series of essays written by people who now feel like telling something of their relationship to the experiments in these unique colleges which lasted a brief year or two—an instant in the educational history of this country—and then dissipated in bickering, disillusion, and, in some cases, collapse.

The book includes student, faculty, and administrative voices. It also represents the perspective offered by the passage of a bit of time since the turbulence, growth, success, and failure we tell of.

What were the dreams which led so many into these five colleges, either to initiate or take part in them? What was the actual reality when the dreams were put into practice (seemingly in every instance so removed from the dream at its conception)? These are questions which, if we have been unable to answer them definitively, have goaded us as we have tried to put back together a tangled, and often bitterly paradoxical, experience with experimental education.

Did adherents of the original dreams for these five colleges decide to cling to the dreams in the face of disaster? Or were the dreams in fact unviable from the beginning, and was the decision made to deal with "facts" such as student interests, atmosphere, structure or non-structure, and so on? These, also, are questions that beg for answers and have motivated much of what is written here.

And what was the joy inherent in trying to provide alternatives to America's educational status quo? For there was, and is, much laughter and happiness in being involved with our five experimental colleges.

One thing seems immediately clear: anyone who has remained an outside observer, no matter how well-informed or friendly, cannot tell this story. It has had to come from those who like ourselves were completely committed to what was going on in these colleges, and therefore have taken a certain responsibility for them and for our behavior in them. Only these people can begin to touch (and perhaps even they cannot convey) the realities of Antioch-Putney, Bensalem, Fairhaven, Franconia, and Old Westbury.

And we also wish to make clear that we are not telling our stories in the spirit of disillusioned moralizing or finger pointing or even out of any desire to draw conclusions about our experiences. If we have been incapable of resisting these temptations, then hopefully we have been judgmental to as minute a degree as humanly possible. For we understand among ourselves that disillusion will not bind us together. What will bind us together is the continued ability—once evidenced in our dedication to our respective colleges—to be sincerely excited by the prospect of improving the human condition and the additional ability to tell others about what we have attempted, the mistakes we have made, the possibilities for further exploration and endeavor.

Given the imperative of freedom, the ideas and realities of freedom as they are revealed in the stories you are about to read, people will not be satisfied. They move on, investigate, begin over and over again to find new and finer directions. They launch themselves into experiments once thought to be heresy. Nothing appears to be left sacred. Yet underlying every conscious action there exists a driving, unconscious desire to sur-

vive, to flourish, to have done with foolishness and to get along
with the business of living life as it *will* be lived—not as it has
been, or ought to be lived—but as it is.

Gary B. MacDonald
Elizabeth Sewell

1 January 1972

Editor's Note

The organizing principle of this book evolved by warp and woof across the country over the telephone, in the shower, over drinks in various watering-holes, in minutes of fretful sleepless-ness, in a flash. Mostly it evolved through serious worrying on the editor's part. All of which may seem absurd to recount, except there is a point. To reiterate how the book was put together is to immediately say a great deal about what is in it, and how it all hangs together.

Every notion of separating the essence of these five colleges into pieces of the whole that could be considered individually has been thrown out—to be replaced with a clear certainty that each essay considers the totality, the *gestalt*, of its subject. In other words each essay in its own way contains dreams, realities, meditations, and a good deal of auxiliary material relevant not only to the particular college at hand but, in most instances, to all of the other colleges as well. Thus each essay is at once speaking not only of itself but of its fellow essays as well. Like-wise, each college is speaking of itself and also of its fellow colleges. Among themselves these essays, quite naturally, set up a curious cross-referencing, checking and balancing, self-criti-cizing and complimenting totality all their own. This means that if, for example, one is pursuing Roy P. Fairfield's "Power to Poetry?" one is in that process getting additional insights into Kenneth Freeman's "Bensalem: An Analysis," and vice versa. All of these essays relate to each other in a variety of ways, a few of them difficult at first to understand. The reader is encouraged to read no one essay as though it were an autonomous unit but as though it were integrally connected at every level to those that surround it.

The "Dreams" and "Realities" sections in each chapter elucidate questions we outlined in the Introduction. The "Dreams" are primarily excerpts from each college's catalog, and the "Realities" are the experiences covered in the essays themselves.

Remember, too, that the one definite suggestion to all of these contributors was that they keep always to the human point of view in their papers; that they each deal with what it was like for them personally to be involved with their respective colleges. The reader might pay special attention to the palpable emotions which surface in every essay. For me, these many emotions constitute the gestalt to be understood before the exigencies of America's experimental college movement can be fathomed—or ignored.

G.B.M.

I Bensalem College

The place immediately took on the characteristics of anarchy and atomism. . . . "Total freedom" became the rallying cry. The Chair found itself responsible and answerable for what happened in a group where any attempt at control was rejected with hostility and accusations of violation of principles.

ELIZABETH SEWELL

DREAMS
Start with People
ELIZABETH SEWELL

The following was written by Elizabeth Sewell in the spring of 1967, before Bensalem opened, for the magazine *Fordham*, an alumni journal. Miss Sewell then moved on to become chairwoman of Bensalem. A poet, critic, and novelist, Miss Sewell has also published numerous essays dealing with education. Two of these are: "First Reports from an Experimental College," *Journal of Applied Behavioral Science*, Volume 4, Number 3, and "Space for Something Else," *New City: Man in Metropolis*, Volume 6, Number 8, August 1968. Presently she resides in New Jersey and teaches at Hunter College in New York City.

The times are revolutionary. Of course they have been since 1642 in my native country and since 1776 in my adopted one, and there is no let-up in sight yet. Hannah Arendt says that when the history of this century, as well as the last, comes to be written it will be threaded by this series of revolutions, but the task cannot be done yet for the thread has yet to run. Certainly if one begins listing (even from an unprofessional memory) the relevant dates, one gets slightly giddy. After the two already mentioned comes 1789 thundering in, then 1830, 1848, 1871, 1917, 1922, 1934, which is Mao Tse-Tung's Long March, 1956 for Hungary and 1958 in Cuba. Whether we regard this series as a hopeful or appalling portent, a portent it surely is.

Revolution to many of us used to be something that happened in other people's countries. This is no longer so. The work, the image, perhaps something akin to the reality, has moved in among us. By 1963 the phrase "the black revolution" was in full currency for the explosions occurring then and since then across the face of America. Present-day happenings in the Roman Catholic Church since Pope John and the Council have been called a revolution. A glance at my bookshelf and I can pick out a paperback entitled *Revolution at Berkeley*, 1964. And the word was used repeatedly, in public too, during a speech in October, 1965, when ground was broken for the new Lincoln Center campus of Fordham University in Manhattan.

Poems and Revolutions

We may see all of these references to revolution as connected, if we choose—part of "that far deeper and more permanent revolution in the moral world of which the recent changes in the political world may be regarded as the pioneering whirl-wind and storms." That is Coleridge in 1817, and for a poet who is thought of as a good safe conservative, he uses the word "revolution" surprisingly often. But then poets, "Makers" as they are known by their ancient name, have a way of winding in and out of revolutions. Milton, our greatest example, begins this series, and it runs on through Blake and Shelley and Petofi and Hugo and Rimbaud (again this list is from rather random memory) and Blok and Mao, who is, one understands, a poet in his own right, and those I can give no names to but who tacked up their poems on the Budapest street corners where they and the young fought against tremendous odds, and died.

After all these great events and great people, it seems ridiculous in the next breath to start talking about a small new beginning which Fordham will launch in the summer of 1967, an

Experimental College in which, this first year, thirty freshmen —men and women—and a small group of faculty will set up house and live and work together. What, one might ask, is revolutionary in that? The answer is, simply, that their intent is to rethink the whole of modern education.

All revolutions start absurdly, but if you want to start one you had best start at the bottom, start small and *start with people*. This is also why I am writing as I am, personally. It would have been possible to introduce this experiment as an attempt to put into practice theories on the nature of education, curriculum, problems, the learning process, etc. But that is not how it started. It started with people.

As a poet I had always found it natural to be interested in revolution. Only gradually, however, has it become clear to me that all such instinctive—that is, living and prophetic—interests of the mind next lead to involvement and action, "the growth and revolutions of an individual mind," a Coleridgean phrase again. I note one or two such revolutions of my own to start with.

The Art of Thinking

The first, and as yet most shattering of them all, happened at Cambridge in England during my fifth year of formal university education. Weary of ploughing through the countless treatises other people had written on my dissertation subject, which was language and poetry in general and late nineteenth century French poetry in particular, I decided on impulse one afternoon in October, 1946, to begin thinking about language and poetry as if no one had ever thought about them before. It was then I made a discovery: I did not know how to think. That is understatement—I had not the remotest idea what thinking was or how even to make a start on it. To analyze, combine, deduce, arrange, select, the full academic and critical technology (I had graduated with First Class Honours and was on my way to a Ph.D.): yes. To think: no. The whole of my past education, and it could hardly have been better in English terms, crumbled at the roots. For months I crawled about trying to discover what thinking was and how to learn to do it at least a little; found it was common to poetry and to the hitherto closed worlds of mathematics and science; plunged into them with delight; and then made a more final discovery—that such an approach and activity were, in the educational system in which I found myself, totally unacceptable. This was what first brought me to America.

I should like to be able to say that the years following this, during which I wrote a good deal and taught in a wide variety of colleges and universities in the United States, led me, through classroom experience, to see the need for a revolution in education. But it wasn't so, at least not directly. Within a pretty rigid educational system this country offers its *faculty* a great deal of freedom in the classroom. I found it possible to flourish and feel free as a teacher within the system, and I am ashamed to admit that the question whether the *student* was equally free or flourishing did not much occupy my mind. Then in 1964 a chance remark by a colleague woke me. The place was Tougaloo College, Mississippi; the time, the busiest part of 1964; the occasion, a faculty breakfast and the speaker, Dr. Borinski, professor of social science. He was saying to us all, "I suppose you realize that ninety-five percent of what you are teaching these students is quite useless to them." It made me mad—and made me think: he might well be right.

"Polis"

The following year I was trying to write a book on education and thinking. It refused to grow, and was accompanied by a series of dreams in which I was caught with a lot of other people inside huge public buildings which were slowly collapsing. Eventually I had to sit back and ask the book and my dreams, "What are you trying to tell me?" After a while the reply came, "You don't want to write a respectable book, you want to make a revolution," with the note added, "And a public one this time." I agreed, though how, when, where were hidden. But I did know with whom—for in my many teaching jobs I had gathered a small but varied group of young friends—undergraduates, graduate students, junior faculty, all under twenty-eight—and they and I had realized that we might have a job to do together some day. This sense of our variousness (we number among ourselves Americans of Irish, Italian and Negro origin, Asian, English, Jewish, Moslem, Catholic, Protestant) and of our geographical separation, which runs at present from Los Angeles to Lahore in Pakistan, and of belonging together made us search for some image of ourselves as a way of understanding what we might be about. We thought of "College," on the slightly comic analogy of the College of Cardinals, and of "Parish." In the end the image which caught us, however, was that of the *polis*, the city but maybe of some new kind for the mid-twentieth century, a scattered, tiny world-wide city, whatever we could make that mean.

And in an actual city, New York, in September, 1965, Father Leo McLaughlin and I met for dinner on one of my flying visits from England during a year of absence. He told me he had been appointed president of Fordham, and then as we talked there came to us, simultaneously we both avow, an idea. I quote now from the letter I wrote a few days later to two of the young friends in the group: "a vision of a project: of making the revolution I want to make, for so does he; of doing this at Fordham; perhaps 100 students, to live and work as a group with their teachers (co-ed throughout), maybe doing a three-year course, not four; to *find out*, students and faculty alike, what education is, what we need in this day and age, how to learn, how to teach and what. I spoke to him of you and the rest of the group, saying I would want you as consultants and some of us might want to come and actually teach in these surroundings; I asked him when I might be free to approach you and the others, tell you of this idea and ask if you would want to be associated with it. He said, 'At once.' (And there was Father saying, 'We might just conceivably succeed in changing the whole face of education,' to which I replied: 'Nothing less than that will be the least use.')"

Fordham Experiment

So the Experimental College starts at Fordham in mid-July, 1967, with its first thirty students and three or four resident faculty. The first year students will mostly come from Fordham's normal intake by invitation and interview. We mean to extend and diversify this in the future, but all entrants have to meet Fordham entrance standards, to facilitate transfer if our experiment doesn't suit them. My group of young friends has become the committee, five men and three women with myself as chairwoman, who will form the nucleus of the faculty.

We cannot say much about our program until the students arrive since they are part of the planning. One or two practical points, however: we are thinking of a three-year degree course, including summers, leading to a B. A. with thirty students admitted each year. Students will have much time, freedom and responsibility in choosing and shaping their own studies without set requirements and credits. We expect to work through tutorials and seminars. Courses of study will be individual, and demanding. Besides the summers we shall be asking everyone for most of their weekends, for real commitment in fact. Obviously so small a faculty as ours cannot offer anything like a full range of academic subject matter, so we shall offer what we know, rather in the medieval fashion, for here too we mean to start with people, and our students will go out into "big" Fordham for the rest of what they want. We hope very much that the faculty will be good to us in our tentative endeavors. It is no part of our plan to be a little separate cell away on our own, and we shall be most grateful for interest, criticism and above all friendliness toward what we are trying to do; agreed, as I take it we all are, that first, a Fordham B.A. degree should designate neither a pedant nor a dilettante, and second, the extent of student disaffection (if that is the right word) throughout the country suggests urgently that we try something.

Probably each of us has some particular approach or clue. My own passion after my Cambridge experience is to have us work at thinking, finding out more of what it is, how to do it, how to encourage it in others and using it as a living and organic basis that holds humanities and science together. This thinking is something different from, though not substituting for or hostile to, the mental technology of logic and order and manipulation which all academics must acquire. (I recall with delight the retired Harvard professor who suddenly burst out when I was describing our Experimental College to him with, "I don't know how to think—I'll come—I'll join.") Others of us have other passions and ideas. There is room here for all who want to help.

People and "Others"

There is more to the *polis*, the revolution under that image, than education, however widely interpreted. As *polis* the experimental college is to be a place where people's lives belong, in friendship and common purpose. It is also a place where *other* people's lives belong. Students everywhere are beginning to ask that their work in classroom and college should relate to their own lives, inner and outer, and to the life of the community where they live. This demand is in itself revolutionary for our universities have continued to work as if today, as in the distant past, men still had to retire from the world and cloister themselves with those like-minded to study and be learned, an ideal which has now grown obsolete. So we expect some of our students in the college may want to go away for a time during their three years to work, say, in a community project at home or abroad (and also, incidentally, to learn or perfect a foreign language), and we would plan for this.

The small *polis* which Fordham is founding here has to bear its share in the greater *polis* beyond it, and beyond this again, in the wider world, West and East of today. Nothing less than this seems adequate to our time. We see the variety and friendship within our committee as one step in this direction. So is our scatteredness, for we have to learn how to build and hold together a small world-city that moves and extends its limits as its citizens move so that wherever any member of our group is, there is the *polis*. We have tried various ways of maintaining close ties, including keeping and exchanging diaries, and I have found outside of the educational world altogether much interest in this side of our experiment, as if communities of this scattered sort might have some importance for the future.

Which brings me to my last point—we are not, and are not going to be, the only ones making this revolution. Many others are making it along with us. Experimental colleges of this kind are springing up all across the country. I have to be in touch with them later to see if we could exchange news, ideas, mistakes, perhaps meet and talk sometime. If this works, it will put Fordham in contact with a number of interesting places. It will show us too, soberingly and encouragingly, that we are not as way-out as we think, that a need for revolution exists everywhere and that it is possible to start again, not with a system or a machine, but with people.

From the Bensalem College Catalog
1968–1969

Just what education for today and tomorrow must involve needs exploring, and that exploration deserves the widest latitude. There are no formal majors or departments at Bensalem. Each student selects one of the faculty as a consultant and works with him and others (consulting committees most commonly include a faculty member and two students) in shaping and reshaping an educational experience. The student is also responsible for keeping a cumulative dossier, records of work and experience, which will fulfill the function of a transcript. Some students concentrate most of their learning in one or two areas, while others spread out more widely. Learning together at Bensalem involves tutorials, seminars (initiated and run by students or faculty or both), independent study, group projects, workshops and countless informal, spontaneous interactions which are part of living together. Students can also, if they wish, take courses in any branch of Fordham University, and many have done so. Members of Fordham's regular faculty have been generous with their time in this respect. Indeed, the whole of the university's facilities (library, recreation, social life and so on) are available to Bensalem students. They have also attended classes at the New School, at the Free School of New York, at the Alternate University and at the "Free University" run by Fordham College students. Attendance at conferences on educational innovation and visits to other experimental colleges and intentional communities have also been part of the picture. Bensalem receives a large number of visitors from all parts of the country, and these visits are seen as part of the educational experience.

Work has been undertaken in the community, in schools, hospitals, organizations concerned with housing and rent problems and so on. A number of Bensalem students have spent a summer in Europe for travel-study and language work. One student worked in a village project in Mexico after a year centered largely on Latin American studies and the learning of Spanish [this student is Rose Calabretta, from whom the reader will hear later—Ed.] and another will spend the summer of 1969 in Lesotho as part of the Crossroads Africa program. Interest in city planning has led still another to compete for and obtain a National Urban Fellowship, becoming one of twenty students who will be working closely with the Mayor of New York City during 1969–70. A group project centering on the question of human rights eventually resulted in two students becoming members of the New York State Division of Human Rights as investigators for the summer. Seven Bensalemites have been working in private and public schools throughout the city as part of their own program of teacher education. For a fuller and more intense communal living experience, a faculty member and a group of students moved to a house on City Island. All of this is encouraged not as "extracurricular" activity but as a full and proper part of university education.

What is being described clearly involves unprecedented freedom and—as one learns soon enough—unprecedented responsibility. Bensalem is an attempt to give reality to the "living and learning community" cliche, to involve everyone as fully as possible in making decisions affecting the community, and to bring together our daily lives, our educations and the world around us in order to act towards good change in ourselves and the world.

Bensalem is not a college only for the very gifted. Its aim is to give much greater scope and freedom than is normally possible today in the highly structured American system of education; it also encourages choice and independence and a commitment to learning which will really mean something to the students themselves and lend much-needed new meaning to today's regulation B.A. degree. Bensalem therefore welcomes a fairly wide range of ability in potential students, and admission is determined almost wholly by interview, conducted by students and faculty jointly. The main qualifications are a readiness to take responsibility for shaping one's own education, a willingness to cooperate in the undertakings of one's fellow-learners, a real interest in education in today's society and in its reshaping, and a commitment to the community and the ideas behind this experiment, as they change and grow with each new group of students and faculty who come to take up the work that is Bensalem.

REALITIES

Bensalem: an Analysis

KENNETII D. FREEMAN

In 1969 Dr. Kenneth Freeman became the director of Bensalem. He
has recently accepted the position of Dean at Fairhaven College, another experimental institution dealt with later in this book. He began
his work at Fairhaven in 1971.

In many ways Bensalem has been the fantasy land of academe.
The tiny college attempted a significant reordering of the
power structure of the modern university. Professors and students have all, in an idle moment, wondered what would happen if the faculty or the university hierarchy had no significant
political power over the student. What if there were no grades,
no requirements? And what if the students controlled the governance of the institution? By design and, more perhaps, by
historical accident Bensalem has taken these questions seriously
and evolved as a college with no requirements beyond a vague
three-year connection with the bursar. There are no grades or
academic checkpoints and even contact with a faculty advisor
may be only *pro forma*. A student may at the end of three years
turn in a statement saying only that he has been enrolled for
three years, and he will receive the B.A. from Fordham Univer-

sity. Not only has the student been given complete academic freedom, but also the government of the college is almost entirely in student hands. Decisions concerning hiring, firing, allocation of funds, and so forth, are all made on a community basis in which the faculty have a vote, but only one vote per person. Thus the power bases of the college, traditionally concentrated within the faculty, have been shifted to the students.

Such a shift is a great threat to traditional faculty members. Wherever I have talked of Bensalem at regular colleges the response from the faculty reveals that the threat is both real and felt. It is clear that more is involved in Bensalem than an experiment with academic freedom. The nature of the university is being questioned. It is certainly not surprising that beginning in the spring of 1971, when Fordham began to consider changes for Bensalem, the primary theme of these changes was a reassertion of the usual power of the faculty over the students. These changes within Bensalem are not complete, but as I write this in the summer of 1971, it is clear that what I say applies to the past only. A college called Bensalem may continue to exist at Fordham University, but it will be a very different place and most of the following comments will not apply. While my comments are in the present tense, they might better be in the past.

I am glad to have been part of Bensalem. I consider it a significant moment in the development of American colleges and think it important that analyses of the college be attempted. Here I shall discuss self-government, the academic program and the faculty. These three hardly exhaust the matter and to comment on them as separate from the totality is highly artificial. Yet the choice is not accidental, for these three focus most of the concern of the traditional university about Bensalem. This is fair, but the analysis distorts the reality of Bensalem for it tends to suppress the moments of joy, happiness and close sense of community and togetherness which occasionally happen. It is always this way: the negative leap out, whereas the positive items are more subtle. It is difficult to chronicle the growth of the human spirit. Thus the comments need to be read with sympathy and understanding. In seeking to break new paths, Bensalem has made many mistakes, and it is easy to come to the conclusion that the approach is just wrong-headed. I for one do not think it is. Having shared its life for two years, I am convinced that in Bensalem exists a more humane and creative form of higher education.

Bensalem is in the Bronx. It is in the middle of a drab tiny street closed at both ends; one block off Fordham Road, a main thoroughfare of the Bronx. It is surrounded by the university and Italian neighbors, and Bensalem has never been sure which of these elements is the more antagonistic to its program. The college is centered in a dilapidated apartment building dating from the turn of the century. The building is cut into twenty apartments which maximize privacy between apartments and minimize it within the apartment—just the reverse of what is needed. The one common room is small and a marvel of disorder. The special facilities of the college are limited to one small darkroom with sparse equipment. The maintenance level has been that customarily expected of slum landlords. There has not been much to bring the community together. There are no common eating facilities, no common classroom or seminar meeting places. We have only the apartments—some occupied by faculty and some by students. About the only factor that brings the community together is self-government and to that we now turn.

The question is, can a group of faculty members and students work together in a relationship of political equality (one person, one vote) to govern themselves in matters affecting the college? The experience at Bensalem does not make me hopeful as to a positive answer. Self-government is to me the least successful aspect of the experiment and accounts for much of the hostility which unfortunately marks daily life at Bensalem. Self-government has degenerated to the point where opposing parties merely shout at each other and where there is no longer a forum for either meaningful communication or working together to find reasonable solutions to common problems. The fact that the college ended its current year with half its needed faculty unhired and without a chief administrator is evidence enough that in addition to fostering hostility, the process is ineffective to the point of institutional suicide. Yet self-government is defended with ultimate seriousness at Bensalem. To a large extent this follows from the extended freedom which students enjoy. In the conventional college various groupings of students arise. However, since no group has any real power to determine the main course of the college, these groups have no reason to compete. At Bensalem the students have the political power to shape much of the structure and milieu of their college experience. This gives to the opinions of each group tremendous weight. It is frequently felt that if one group wins, then another group will be excluded from the college and vice versa. This is a fairly accurate perception. While no one can be expelled from Bensalem, students have control of admissions. Thus the dominant group can gradually extend their political base.

Self-government has been through three basic metamorphoses in the three years of the college's life. From the beginning there was the rhetoric of participatory democracy and of self-determination. However, the first government structure had significant exceptions to the scope of this self-determination. For example, in the first year matters of budget and faculty hiring received only scant attention by the students and were largely decided by the director and faculty. For many reasons, tensions grew and led in the second year to a reorganization of the governance of the house. The college divided into two groups, one opting to rule themselves by consensus and the other by majority rule. The division worked well enough until it became necessary for the whole house to make a decision together. Unfortunately, because the procedure for making a joint decision such as the hiring of a new faculty member had not been clarified, it was insisted that when the house got together consensus be the procedure. Bensalem interpreted consensus as the Polish-veto system. That is, any one person who disagreed could block a decision. Along with this development, involvement of the entire community in decision making grew. However, I was the only person hired using this system.

The majority form of government broke down when the consensus group was unable to arrive at a consensus and in effect divided, leaving three groups in the house. Furthermore the community was at that point trying to decide upon a faculty member, and while it was clear that there was overwhelming support for a certain person, there was not 100 percent support. By a variety of moves the community moved to its third and present form of decision-making.

This form of self-government centers in a weekly administrative meeting. An agenda is posted for this meeting and the meeting is attended by those interested. An attempt is made to decide matters by consensus. If it is impossible to arrive at a consensus, then anyone can move the matter to a house meeting, usually held a week later. At the house meeting a 75 percent vote of those present carries. The matter is usually resolved at the house meeting, although if as many as one-fourth of the house wishes, the question goes to a ballot vote of the entire house where it is resolved by 75 percent of those voting. With small numbers the 75 percent requirement means that a friendship group can usually block any proposal. As a rule it only takes eight votes to stop a proposal at Bensalem. Since almost anyone has seven friends, we have not in a very real sense moved far from the consensus method.

By setting the majority at 75 percent, Bensalem still endorses the utopian vision that there is a common ground between people and that rationality and goodwill are sufficient to find that common ground. Little in Bensalem's experience indicates that this is the case. On the contrary, there is ample evidence that there are nonreconcilable differences within the college and that these differences are not going to be solved by discussion. Another obvious aspect of self-government at Bensalem is that it is a game largely without rules. In such a situation those with individual power and individual gifts of rhetoric and persuasion tend to rise to the top of the heap. Self-government becomes the law of the jungle in which control goes to the strong. The weak, or those who for any reason choose not to play in such a chaotic game, are manipulated and controlled by the few who in the best establishment fashion use power ruthlessly. From the standpoint of the few who have worked the Bensalem system to their advantage, it is a very successful system. Thus the power centers in the house are entrenched and determined not to allow any change in the modes of self-government.

The present form of self-government is the most conservative form of government I can imagine. Its dynamics point to a continuation of the status quo. Practically any change is going to hurt someone, and those whom it may hurt would have enough friends to block the change. This means that there is little likelihood that Bensalem, left to itself, would undergo any fundamental alterations.

It is a mistake to construe self-government at Bensalem as a forum for discussion or as anything analagous to the New England town meeting. Indeed, our self-government has become much more theater than forum. For months no significant communication has taken place at a house meeting. Rather, individual groups perform their carefully rehearsed plans for themselves and for each other. A minority of the college still holds to the thin hope that the meetings may be transformed so that people can come together in openness to work, to learn from each other and to find reasonable and common solutions. Regularly, those of such opinions become discouraged, disillusioned and stop coming to house meetings, thus leaving the self-government process an open game for those who harbor no such aspirations.

Self-government at Bensalem consumes the time and energy of the community to a disproportionate degree. This is particularly true for the faculty. To a considerable extent the creative energy of the community is exhausted by the governmental processes, and people are so taxed with the concerns of the process that they become nervous and drained. Further, the hostilities generated through the decision-making process carry over into all aspects of the college. It is rare to find a student working with a professor with whom he politically disagrees. Furthermore, this constant drain upon one's energies produces little result. It would perhaps be worth it if there were any evidence that seniors gain in political understanding. But on the contrary, there is little indication that those who survive the process for three years are any more humane, any more given to working out compromises, any more kind and considerate in regard to individual differences than those who had first entered. Indeed, it seems to be just the reverse. By the time people have been at Bensalem for an extended period of time, any minor disagreement escalates to full scale ideological battle between the forces of good and evil. Perspective is lost and people are dominated by concerns which are genuinely trivial. It is convenient in discussing Bensalem with outsiders to stress that the political process is part of the education Bensalem affords. Certainly this is the case, but it's an open question what end that education serves.

Corresponding to these characteristics of governance is a growing fantasy in the community with regard to the limits of its decision-making powers. Many of the students live in what is now a firm fantasy that they have power not only over Bensalem but indeed over all Fordham and possibly even the universe. This belief is unshaken even by the knowledge that Bensalem does not hire faculty members but rather recommends individuals for Fordham to hire; that Bensalem does not set a budget but rather recommends one; that Bensalem does not have the power to cancel or renew a contract; that Bensalem does not own, maintain or have full authority over its building. The point here is a serious one. Bensalem in reality must function within a framework of givens, both from Fordham and its location. To the extent that this framework is not acknowledged by the participants in the self-government process, an aura of unreality about the entire transaction develops. For example, if Fordham does not accept a budget recommendation from Bensalem then there is, on the part of many students, a keen sense of offense and, indeed, of betrayal. Any attempt to remind the house of the external limitations is taken as a "fascist" trick, evidence of "pig" mentality or subservience to repressive authority.

A kind of anarchism pervades Bensalem's governance; there is no definition of the college or any overarching framework within which to argue a decision. If a student asks for funds for an activity, no statement of the college's purpose exists which would even allow a discussion as to whether or not the request is reasonable. There is not even any agreement as to what constitutes an educational request. In the absence of any such controlling definitions, all matters tend to come down to personalities. Frequently it appears that if the individual proposing something has friends, he gets what he wishes, and if not, his request is ignored. We have neither history nor a constitution to give us a sense of objective reality.

A major aspect of Bensalem self-government is faculty hiring. We have a method which makes almost no sense, for it requires the individual to be interviewed and ultimately approved by 75 percent of the community and results in merely a gigantic popularity contest. The process now resembles the election of a local sheriff: each group in the community tries to get a faculty member sympathetic to its interest. With this method it is impossible to agree upon areas of need or even upon the kind of person that one is looking for. Such criteria vary with individuals. The result is usually a stalemate, and it has been over a year since a faculty vacancy was filled despite the fact that we are overwhelmed with candidates who wish to become faculty members. To be fair the process worked in its first year to secure three new faculty members.

There is another problem here. Usually a faculty member can be hired at Bensalem only by becoming politically allied with one of the groups in the house. There then develops, usually before the faculty member arrives, an intense love affair between a group of students and this particular faculty member. The faculty member is championed by this group and is made to appear the salvation for all the ills of the college. He is supported at the house meetings with praise so extravagant that no committee of ten humans could possibly realize all these campaign promises. When the new faculty person arrives, it is quickly seen that he or she is after all only human, has definite limits to his or her time and energy and cannot supply the motivation and interest missing in the students. At best the faculty member may be a resource person or model, but he or she will not solve the alienation, the loneliness and lack of direction so frequently found at Bensalem. This lack causes the sharpest and most bitter breakup, particularly enervating to the teacher and accounts to a large extent for the student's disillusionment with the faculty.

While I cannot outline an appropriate form of decision-making, it is nevertheless quite clear to me that the present form is a failure. In an attempt to make a radical break from traditional education, Bensalem has ended up time and again *remaking* the mistakes of the traditional system. This is particularly-obvious with respect to self-government. The attempt was to be revolutionary, to create a more humane way of living together and solving mutual problems, yet the reality is that the community has constructed a system which is an exercise purely in power. It is a system where might is right, where intimidation is the standard, where character assassination and abusive rhetoric are common, where self-seeking is the order of the day and where human dignity frequently is nonexistent. No political order in a "corrupt establishment organization" could be less humane, less loving or more illustrative of extreme individualism in pursuit of self-interest.

I am convinced, however, that self-government at Bensalem is not a prerequisite for the academic and social freedom which the place exhibits. This conclusion should be kept constantly in mind as basic to the following discussion of Bensalem's academic side. The word "academic" isn't quite correct; however, I do not know a better phrase for those activities traditionally honored and rewarded in regular colleges, the activities usually referred to as the curriculum. Bensalem is a self-conscious attempt to expand the meaning of this core of education as well as to revalue other aspects of human growth as equally important.

Let me clarify by delineating the three main styles or philosophies of education found at Bensalem. I will overstate these philosophies, but I am sure that one could find "purist" adherents of each in the college. First there is the philosophy, held by a considerable group of faculty and students, that the goals of Bensalem are to be more or less those of a traditional college. This group sees Bensalem as simply an alternative means of realizing the same end. Without too much distortion this end can be labeled graduate school preparation. The group tends to be oriented toward the traditional disciplines, even among those who are open to inter-disciplinary work. The approach centers upon learning the methods and skills of the academic trade. Those holding this philosophy have no quarrel, then, with the usual goals of the university, but they feel that the restrictions and the lockstep of the traditional university get in the way of learning, and they wish to have freedom to go about the task in the proper way.

A second philosophy defines the end of undergraduate education in terms of the total person and sees the point of the college experience to be a maturing process in which one undergoes the transition from adolescent to adult. It is primarily an emotional change which may include cognitive elements. However, the cognitive elements are definitely subordinate to the emotional, moral and spiritual aspects. This philosophy is prone to be expressed as "getting oneself together" or finding "where one's head is at." Despite lip service paid to this ideal in the usual college catalog, this approach is an offense to much of contemporary academia. It is, oddly enough, a harking back to the old denominational academies of the nineteenth century. It is, I think, also a direct reaction to the sterility of the contemporary discipline-oriented university.

The third philosophy of undergraduate education seen at Bensalem is difficult to describe without prejudice. This philosophy sees the college as primarily a haven or a sanctuary in which one may escape for a period of time from the absurdities of the contemporary world. Those endorsing such a philosophy know very well that they are in college purely because of societal and parental demands and that to them the usual ways of interpreting college make no sense. The one function the college may serve is to be a protective barrier between them and the world. Such an approach to education places minimal demands upon the school, but one demand vigorously advanced is that infringement of the college upon the student's individual life be minimal. This philosophy is also regularly found in the traditional college.

In listing these three philosophies of education present at

Bensalem I wish to stress that I do not consider any of them in principle absurd. Given the exigencies of our contemporary society, a solid philosophical case can be erected for any one of the three. I, by training and temperament, tend to go toward the first; nevertheless, I am keenly aware that this is to a large extent the end of education which is being attacked in our contemporary world, and that the university has strong need to experiment not only with alternative means but with alternative ends to the undergraduate process. Even superficial reflection will reveal that an openness to alternative ends for education will have far-reaching and often unexpected results.

With such divergent philosophies held by students and faculty, an evaluation of the academic program of the college is difficult, if not impossible. The academic aspects of Bensalem are, therefore, genuinely in chaos, but it must be stressed again that this chaos is possibly Bensalem's real strength. Such a state is a far cry from the usual experiment where one has pre-selected ends and then attempts to determine whether or not a given method will bring about these ends. The academic chaos precludes systematic analysis, but a few observations are in order.

One of the outstanding characteristics of Bensalem is that, compared to the regular colleges, it is a more honest approach to education. Students have described the experience as walking around with a mirror constantly before you. In a traditional college, the framework frequently allows one to fool himself into thinking that he is performing satisfactorily. Many students do no academic work until the night before the exam, and they either cram in enough to pass or visit the fraternity files. They work the system and get their "C," and yet they have accomplished very little, and what is worse, they have never been brought up against their own lack of accomplishment. At Bensalem if the student is working and producing, it is obvious; and if he is not, there is no incentive to fool anyone into thinking he is. It is my judgment that the actual amount of academic learning and work at Bensalem is not markedly different from that in a traditional college. However, the appearance is vastly different because those at Bensalem who are not engaged in learning are quite obviously not engaged. Parenthetically, this poses severe adjustment problems for Bensalem's professors. Although they should know better, college professors frequently deceive themselves into thinking that all of their students are studying and learning. At Bensalem one confronts the student without his academic Sunday dress on, and the experience can be genuinely disquieting.

At a recent conference someone reported on a study which contended that in the traditional college roughly a third of the students were genuinely interested in learning and studying along lines traditionally defined, and the rest in varying degrees were working the system to get the B.A. This statistic proves to be roughly accurate for Bensalem. That is, in my judgment about one-third of the students have a serious desire to learn along traditional lines. For this third Bensalem is clearly a very good place. It gives them the freedom to structure their lives in accord with their interests; it provides them with superb counselling and an emotional support framework for learning. For such students it is the best educational experience of which I can conceive. Understandably, this group accounts for Bensalem's unusually high success rate in getting its graduates into prestigious graduate schools with handsome fellowships. It is for the other two-thirds of the students that questions of an academic nature become difficult to answer. It is certainly arguable that three years of confronting themselves in Bensalem provides students with a greater educational and moral experience than four years of playing the system for what it's worth. Also, with regard to the retention of information, it is not clear that Bensalem would be behind the regular college. Bensalem students learn much from their contact with each other and from the faculty. They tend to become interested in something and read extensively in that area. I certainly would not be surprised if testing were to reveal that Bensalem seniors scored as high on retention of information as students from a regular college, but I would say that this is less a compliment to Bensalem than it is a critique of those who measure colleges by such standards.

In very concrete terms one way to judge the academic program is by the number of students who work closely with faculty. For example, one objective criterion might be the amount of time that students spend working with faculty. But notice that while this is perhaps a great virtue for those endorsing the second philosophical position (where the college is seen as a transition ritual and there is a great need for emotional models), nevertheless, for either the first or third philosophies (the college as academic preparation for graduate school or the college as a sanctuary), there is no particular need for much consultation with the professor. We also know that, given motivation and a good library, one can learn without professors. (The above comments are theoretical; in practice, it is the first group which uses the faculty.) In any event, it is my informal observation that of the sixty-five students officially connected with the college last year, approximately sixteen worked very closely with a faculty member. That is, they were in regular detailed consultation with the professor concerning their work and studying with the professor in a variety of areas. At the other end of this particular spectrum, I would say that approximately thirteen of our students had no significant contact with faculty members during the year. The rest of the students fall in between. However, it is probably the case that at least half the students have only minimal contact with the faculty. Furthermore, if one examines the students who are involved in group projects at Bensalem, the seventeen who worked closely with the professors account for almost all the students involved.

A comment about the students who work closely with the

professors: it is not surprising that by and large these are the students who the professors liked best. There has been a mutual selection process. Students who work closely with the faculty tend to be those normally associated with honors programs in the regular college. They are bright, articulate, highly individualistic, self-motivated and self-disciplined. Of the three philosophies of education discussed earlier, they belong almost exclusively to those who see the college as an academic place.

Yet all Bensalem students are bright, articulate, and individualistic. Given the last attribute especially, it is difficult to get them to understand the need for a responsibility within the group to shared learning. That is, that the Bensalem community, out of a necessity created by its own internal dynamics, pursue certain common learning goals, no matter how boring or irrelevant these goals may seem to particular individuals. Common learning goals may be a knowledge of history, for example, or even knowledge of more specific subjects, of greater contemporary interest, perhaps, such as racism, aggression, revolution and so on. But the students are far more like a typical professor who, if he is not interested in studying a subject, will not study it, than they are like the typical student who occasionally studies things he does not find interesting either because someone else thinks he should or because of the demand of the study group. I find this individualism and lack of group responsibility distressing; nevertheless I realize these students are only copying the professional models of American academe.

One of the problems of the Bensalem approach is that there is no specific and regular mechanism for encouraging the student to expand his intellectual horizons. In the traditional college a move is made in this direction by means of requirements which force the student to sample a variety of intellectual disciplines. The freedom at Bensalem makes it possible for the student to continue only those interests he had upon finishing high school. Bensalem tends to be a way of moving the specialization of graduate school down into the undergraduate level. In theory the individual student's work should lead him to explore a variety of intellectual involvements. Sometimes the theory works; as a rule it does not.

One glaring characteristic of Bensalem's academic program is the absence of innovative, experimental teaching methods. The technique used thus far between the students and faculty is among the oldest known in the academic world. Primarily it involves seminars and tutorials. Exciting and unusual ways of presenting material are largely nonexistent. The Lorillard Children's School stands as one possible exception to this statement. (The School being a project in which several Bensalem students participate—Ed.) There the principle of learning by doing is practiced. While this is certainly not a new idea, it is nevertheless exciting and infrequently seen in the academic world. There are many reasons for the nonexperimental nature of the teaching process at Bensalem. In the first place, the initiative to learn falls upon the student, whereas many of the new and exciting techniques used elsewhere are aimed at supplying motivation by making the material more palatable for the student. Another reason is the lack of a predictable number of students in the group. It is not at all unusual for a group of fifteen or so students at the start of a project to drop to three or four. Given the unpredictable make-up of the group, one is frequently unable to plan and realize many exciting possibilities. A third very important reason for the absence of innovative teaching techniques is that many expectations of a faculty member at Bensalem focus upon the general life and not upon the classroom. Thus a great deal of energy goes into the day by day living with students. Few professors have the time and energy left to think of innovative teaching methods. These reasons are probably not sufficient, but they at least point to a real problem: that experimentation at Bensalem is totally related to the *structure* of the college and not related to its educational content.

In short, Bensalem is a miniature multiversity except that student interests are allowed to run wild without any effort to channel them. As a result among the fifty-plus students one would find literally hundreds of interests. There is, consequently, no way for a small group of faculty to meet these interests. Thus one usually finds a teacher overworked while dealing with only a small group of students. Yet, correspondingly, many students see the teacher as worthless simply because the professor's interests are not their's and because he has so little time for them. In this kind of situation the tutorial approach is wrong-headed. No college today can afford the student-faculty ratio which allows for an effective tutorial program.

The relationship between faculty and students of Bensalem tends to mirror patterns found in the traditional university. Students look for faculty members to support their pursuits, a behavior trait which, in the university setting, has probably helped to fortify the already impregnable academic departments. ("If a student is interested in ethics, then of course we in the philosophy department are best equipped to assist him," and so on.) What is needed, on the other hand, is less attention to the specific interests of students and faculty members and more attention to finding faculty members who can listen well and critically and can facilitate the intellectual-emotional growth of the students, even across markedly different academic interests. Locating such faculty members is difficult. (Even if one locates them, getting them hired is next to impossible!) By and large Bensalem has attempted to provide an experimental framework of education and yet has continued to use faculty members trained and motivated in traditional ways. The combination is not particularly happy. Unfortunately, there is no place for appropriately trained people to turn in the academic community. One finds them by accident, if at all. Here again Bensalem mirrors the problems of the general academic community. Even those faculty members who have reacted strongly against contemporary university patterns are nevertheless so involved with them that they find it difficult to escape.

Supposedly at the heart of the Bensalem approach is the academic counselling program. In theory the faculty and students live together, and from these informal contacts come ample opportunities for discussion of all phases of a student's life. For those students who take advantage of these theoretical possibilities it is truly an exceptional opportunity to have a close working relationship with a variety of faculty members. Unfortunately most students do not take advantage of this aspect of Bensalem and certainly less than half of the students have any sustained counselling relationship with a faculty member. In one sense it is a good thing; were all the students to enter into close relationships with faculty members, the faculty would be overworked to the point of exhaustion. It is probably only because most of the students do not choose such relationships that the faculty has the time and energy to do a good job with those who do.

One other aspect of the academic program needs to be highlighted. There is a tendency in experimental situations for the faculty to be slowly excluded. Bensalem's faculty has stayed longer and in closer contact with the experiment than might have been expected. Before coming to college, the student normally has three or four different centers of authority over his life to which he must relate. There is the school, his parents, his peer group and sometimes the church. Coming to Bensalem, a student suddenly discovers that he must relate to only one of the four: his peer group. It is perfectly possible to exclude the school as a center of authority in any of the usual senses. This gives the peer group enormous power and makes it very nearly impossible to be a nonconformist in the Bensalem context. People quickly find the subgroup in which they are comfortable, and they rarely deviate from the opinions of that sub-group. Such an approach runs the grave danger of people staying essentially where they were when they came. It also not only runs the risk but has the actual result that people of different and conflicting opinions almost never have occasion for genuine exchange of views. In the traditional college the classroom, for all of its ills, at least brings together a variety of people, in some sense randomly selected, to discuss a common concern. There is a potentiality, frequently realized, for different perspectives to influence each other. This rarely occurs at Bensalem. The cliques are entrenched, and while they may shout at each other, they rarely talk with each other.

One may conclude that Bensalem is an opportunity for an extremely rich experience for those who take advantage of it. That many of the students choose not to avail themselves should be neither surprising nor upsetting. It is also a distinct criticism of Bensalem that it does so little work for those students not academically inclined. Any college can do well, given students who are bookish and wish to study. The challenge in higher education today is to forge ways of working with the students who do not find a place for themselves inside the usual academic context. With the exception of one or two individual faculty members, Bensalem has done very little in this regard.

Much has been said already concerning the faculty and its role in the discussion of the academic aspects of Bensalem. It is appropriate to focus now directly on the faculty. The pattern is rather consistent. We come full of enthusiasm, yet as quickly leave, often with bitterness. In the three years of its existence, Bensalem's faculty turnover has been well over 100 percent. Such rapid turnover and disillusionment is a complex phenomenon, yet one well worth examining. The causes are many and difficult to locate, but certain aspects have become increasingly obvious.

One is the strain of sharing residence with students. The life styles of most faculty members have subtle contrasts to that of contemporary college students. Putting the faculty member into an adolescent community poses problems. Though each problem in itself is small, the total effect is troublesome. Examples might be the noise level or the tendency of students to want to bullshit with you or the frequency with which laundry soap is borrowed. Such small items mount up and begin to grate on faculty nerves. It shows up first and most rapidly on those faculty members who are married. The effort to combine family life with the shared life of a living-learning environment is almost impossible. This is especially true where there are children.

A second problem is that students are frequently omnivorous with respect to faculty time. As an aggregate they will take up as much time as the faculty member is willing to allow. Perhaps any one student would choose only to spend a half-hour a day with a given professor, but there are perhaps thirty or forty who, in a free situation, might choose to spend a half-hour with that professor. This is conjoined with pressures which the faculty members feel they have to be available to students and to have an open door policy. However, very quickly the realities of the situation make themselves felt, and faculty members find themselves cutting the students off: in one way or another making a private space for themselves. Students then often feel hurt and deserted, which further adds to the problem. If he is not very careful the faculty member quickly loses control of his day and among other things finds himself unable to study, which is essential if he is going to do more than simply work off the top of his head. The result for many faculty members is that in a living-learning environment they end up having actually less contact with a large group of students than they do in the regular college environment. The typical pattern within Bensalem is for the faculty member to come to know three or four students very deeply and to have only a casual relationship with the rest. One of the great surprises for me in coming to Bensalem was to discover that faculty members at a small regular college have more genuine contact with students than in Bensalem's living-learning situation. I found that working in a small college, I would frequently seek out the students. I would go to their dorms and their apartments; I would share coffee breaks with them, and I had an office which was quite regularly filled with students. In addition, in a given semester I was teaching forty to fifty students in classes, which provided a base whereby I came to know them. Furthermore, it doesn't seem to me that the relationship between the faculty and the few students with whom they work closely is any deeper at Bensalem than in the small college. Contrasted with the impersonality of the large university, the degree of interaction between the students and faculty at Bensalem is much greater. Contrasted, however, with a good liberal arts college, it has nothing at all to brag about.

Thus the many virtues supposed to flow to the college as a result of faculty and students living together seem to me in the main not forthcoming. In theory the students and faculty learn from each other, observe each other's way of life and in general influence each other through natural and spontaneous interactions. In fact it does not work out this way. The faculty member is but an abstraction to most students and is dismissed by them. Most faculty do not enter deeply into the student peer groups. They are simply residents of the same apartment house.

A related problem here is that a faculty member often feels the need for a platform, a place or situation where he can present in an organized way the results of his learning. With its stress upon conversation, Bensalem seldom affords this opportunity. The tutorial more naturally suits this form of education; it appears a logical outgrowth of sharing a life together. Yet the method is a trap. Two or three eager students can take up the total working time of two or three faculty members. Moreover, a faculty member, even at best, cannot adequately prepare more than five or six tutorials within the course of the week. Clearly, a great many students are left out. The inability to realize the potentialities of the tutorial method, and the frustration which comes from trying, is thus responsible for some of the faculty discontent.

Most faculty members come to Bensalem out of negative reactions to the established institutions and with high hopes and expectations of what Bensalem will afford. The reality of Bensalem is regularly a great shock and disappointment—one with which they frequently are not able to deal successfully. Why this might be so leads to another aspect of the faculty problem.

From what has been said, it is clear that faculty members often see themselves as overworked, harried and in general frustrated by their jobs. Yet, working with only a few students, I think it is less the case that they are overworked than it is that they are in a situation which has relatively little psychological pay-off for them. Faculty members generally are bookish types who enjoy the life of the mind and who have been accustomed to expect a certain kind of psychic pay-off. Given a regular classroom (much like they had in graduate school) and even a small group of interested students, the papers, tests, results, analytic ability and a heightened level of argument quickly follow. These give the professor great satisfaction and transform his work into pleasure. For faculty with these expectations (often hidden even to themselves), Bensalem is a disaster. There are almost no conventional ways of getting these regular pay-offs. One lives a life primarily dictated by the students. He spends his time conversing about things students are interested in, engaged in political processes where the students have the power and often the wisdom, and in general conducting his life far more like a camp counselor than the traditional college professor. Unfortunately, he is not trained to get satisfaction from camp counselor activities.

The students demand from a faculty member, implicitly and explicitly, a mode of living more analogous to that of a pastor or priest than that of the traditional teacher. The demand is to become involved in a loving, supportive relationship with students. It is frequently more important that the professor be "one of the boys" on recreational trips than that he has some learning to impart. In indirect ways the students seek in the lives of faculty members the embodiment of the ideals of the experiment. It is something like a small town where the citizens forbid the pastor to smoke but smoke themselves.

Being a faculty member at Bensalem calls for a fresh notion of leadership. The faculty member as the dispenser of information and knowledge has little place. Needed is rather the faculty member who is a good conversationalist and can work in an informal relationship to facilitate the learning process. The temptation to overlead is resisted with the result that often the faculty doesn't lead at all and leaves everything up to the students. In this situation students are confronted with all the responsibilities of any choice. Often, too keen a sense of the consequences of any decision results and the students opt for a nonthreatening path. This is then a disappointment to the faculty member and he is tempted once more to become the leader. The conflicts are many and intense and involve the total personality.

People with the needed skills for working within Bensalem are not being trained in the contemporary American graduate school, and if one locates a winner, it is by grace and not by plan. Discipline is far less significant than the ability to listen. Overt skills are less important than the subtle ability to facilitate the growth of the student without making him dependent upon you. One needs people with skills, but it is vital that their per-

sonalities not be defined in terms of these skills. Furthermore,
it is almost impossible to escape the American graduate school
without absorbing a keen sense of one's status and importance.
The graduate is prone to feel himself the rightful heir to a
tradition of faculty aristocracy. Such is altogether out of place
within Bensalem. Yet it is difficult to produce new types over-
night. Again Bensalem tries to pour new wine into old wine-
skins.

Perhaps the faculty is not necessary to education; I'm certainly willing to entertain the hypothesis that for a certain kind
of education a faculty in the traditional role is not needed.
However, in our present world a faculty must be involved in the
academic process if the school is to survive as a degree-granting
college. I am convinced that attitudes toward teachers at Bensalem are increasingly observable in American colleges. To this
extent these difficulties discussed above are not local in nature,
but rather express a genuine and deep need for a different kind
of faculty member. Methods of selection, training, recruitment
and evaluating must be devised. Mere goodwill is insufficient.

In discussing three aspects of Bensalem (self-government,
academic program and the faculty) the focus has been upon the
negative—upon the problems, upon pitfalls to be addressed and
if possible avoided in moving in the direction of experimental
education. As I look over the words here, I am impressed at how
different the reality is from my arid analysis of it. Where in these
dire sentences would one find the reality of a student who came
to Bensalem, coped with his freedom, solved a drug problem
and became a self-directed classic scholar good enough to be
going to the University of Chicago on a Danforth Fellowship?
Where is contained the story of a girl who has discovered and
strengthened her many talents as a disciplined actress? These
realities and many like them are lost, and my comments are
weakened thereby. My only defense is that I was not attempt-

ing a description of Bensalem, but rather an analysis of some of its many facets. My hope is that my comments will serve to further this style of education and not act as ammunition to those who believed all along that such a program would not work.

Beyond the Old and the New

ROSE CALABRETTA

> . . . for we are beyond both the old world and the
> new.
>
> FRANCIS BACON
> *New Atlantis*

A graduate of Bensalem, Rose Calabretta is a woman who travels a
great deal: various reports place her in the Dominican Republic, Mexico, and India. Nevertheless, her home base continues to be New York
City

When I arrived at Bensalem in July 1967, I hadn't the slightest
idea what we would do. I did not know what education was, nor
had I ever thought of what an educational revolution might be.
And now, looking back on those crucial first days and indeed on
three years of the experiment, I seriously doubt that any of us
had considered these things, and I am certain that none of us
could possibly have dreamt of what was actually to take place
under the slogan and guise of a "living and learning community."

Of course I speak as student, but in Bensalem I often found myself (as did we all) playing the roles of teacher and administrator as well, depending on the particular time, place and incident which changed as constantly and unpredictably as in Alice's Wonderland, and just as fearfully. I prefer not to point fingers or place the blame for the entire endeavor on any one person or on American society as a whole. I seek only to describe what we tried to do, what I saw happen and what I have done. With this purpose in mind, I have divided the experience into the public sphere which we all shared in the experiment, and the private sphere in which I lived in solitude and with my friends, and of course I have qualified the account according to my individual vision and perception.

Bensalem's first year could be described as a naïve and abortive attempt to establish a working community and begin an educational revolution. Among Bensalem members, reference is often made to the "Wednesday Revolution" which took place on the third day of our existence. I remember being awakened early that morning by loud pounding on my door and shouts of "Revolution!" and being led to our basement common room where a written schedule was ceremoniously ripped up. The piece of paper was an innocent attempt to arrange the day according to topic meetings which we had planned with faculty the previous day. It became the symbol of "them, out there," meaning everything we had abandoned as "educational revolutionaries." I was stunned. I did not know what was happening nor what should have been happening, and no one made any motion to contradict what was taking place. On this third day all order and hope of success was ripped up along with the schedule.

Shortly after the revolution's revolution, it became quite evident that all of us were not present at Bensalem for the same reason, and we found ourselves divided, including faculty, into two main factions: one favoring a "learning community" and

another defining itself as a "living community." This split became increasingly rigid and volatile over the public issues of
discipline and academic criteria. Our political dilemma began
with trying to work out a way to live together, but out of fear
of all regulations, we left simple living rules like noise control,
for example, to individual discretion in the spirit of "love and
trust." Unfortunately, we found that one individual's sense of
discretion differed, at times radically, from another's. During
that first year I found myself sandwiched between a bass guitar
and its sister, the melody, who practiced most any hour of the
day and night. I was forced out of my apartment to the university library in order to accomplish the bulk of my serious work.
I moved out of the main building for the remaining two years.
Problems of noise, animals, drugs, dirt and more were never
settled, either.

The problem of academic criteria existed on many levels: we
had to deal with the extreme anxieties of the so-called academicians concerning the risk involved with entering the public
academic world after three years of private experimentation;
also present was the open terror of the communitarians at being
faced with competition and possible failure in or exclusion from
the larger world outside Bensalem. Objectively, however, the
academic criterion was the validity of one's chosen work during
the short space of three years.

Discipline and academic criteria endured as problems the
entire first three-year period at Bensalem and opened our eyes
to the paralyzing reality that we had no way to make decisions
about them. Which is to say, all of our decisions were made on
the basis of a unanimous vote. There was no reason for adopting
such a decision-making process; it was simply a natural move on
our part to give each person an equal say in all matters, allowing
no authoritative or definitive status to faculty or to anyone else.
We very quickly realized that this made the entire body subject

to the tyranny-of-one regarding all decisions. These decisions ranged from the simple determination of the deadline for incoming applications to the more complex and important matters of the apportionment of annual funds and the procedure for interviewing and admitting new students and faculty members. In general we discussed an issue until we reached unanimous nervous exhaustion and the matter was sufficiently simplified to satisfy all members, and therefore stated absolutely nothing. We settled the matter of academic transcripts in this way, ending with the phenomenal declaration that each of us had to maintain a relationship with one faculty member with whom we must invent a written document to describe all that we had accomplished in three years. If the student could not maintain a satisfactory relationship with one faculty member, he could look for another who would better understand him and his particular interests. In other words, a student could do anything he wished for three years as long as he could find someone to call his adviser. This naturally affected the decisions made about faculty appointments.

The political situation became deadlocked between two unmoving groups, and we could find no remedy for our political paralysis until the summer between the second and third years, when our newly-hired director suggested and somehow had passed the proposal to settle all deadlocked decisions on the basis of a 75 percent majority house vote. This appeared to settle the two-year chaos in which we had been living, but it did not rule out the possibility of reversing a previously held decision to suit the present and pressing occasion, even if the decision had just been settled the week or the day before. The chaos in the administrative realm grew as the years went on with no hope of introducing any stability. After a very short time all decisions became a contest of point-scoring between factions. Political activity reached the point of ridiculousness when students began to apply for faculty positions to alleviate their personal financial situations and wield increased power, and when applicants to Bensalem were admitted by the only student who appeared at the interview who just happened to be the brother, sister or friend of the person who desperately needed to be a part of the experiment. At this time during the third year, so many friends of students were living in our main building that it was nearly impossible to know who was and who was not a student: that is, who had paid tuition and who had not.

There are many incidents which could be recounted about the administrative difficulties of the group because we never determined a firm decision-making policy upon which we could all agree for a reasonable amount of time. We evolved through various stages of political disagreements for the sake of discovering a viable means to settle common matters, but in none of these stages did anyone have the power to make decisions and carry us on to greater and more important matters, such as the nature of education. The faculty took no power, and we as a group gave them no authority. Bensalem seemed born this way, and this is the way we killed ourselves as well.

It was this aspect, the absence of authority, that made the public sphere of Bensalem life more a living hell than a suitable educational environment. The complete absence of traditional roles threw the entire burden of education into the hands of the individual, making the teaching-learning experience a private, untouchable sphere of one's life, as opposed to the social experience we usually define education to be. Ideally, I imagine that freedom of choice was intended as a response to the empty irrelevance of assigned subject matter in the naïve hope that choice would make things relevant. This was clearly not the case. Rather, the undefined atmosphere tended to confuse and paralyze the student. Seminars and tutorials were held at any hour of the day or night, and one was free to come or to go elsewhere as he wished. This "absolute freedom" allowed for the infamous one-week or one-day long seminars which simply fizzled out for lack of interest in the substance of the proposed topic. It also provided the space necessary for year-long, self-structured inquiry seminars which demanded shared responsibility from both faculty and students to organize and present the chosen material. Many students did not know what they wanted to do; many skipped from one major field of interest or concentration to another in hopes of finding something which would interest them. The question of what we were to study and how we would go about it was totally our private responsibility, and many times it led to the absurd realization that one had no real interests at all and was bored with himself. In despair students often became totally dependent upon faculty for academic direction. This dependence on someone older for the proper educational prescription might easily be traced to the structured, dictatorial system from which we had graduated in high school, but such an acknowledgement did not fill the educational vacuum in which we found ourselves.

In telling the story of my own education, I would have to say that Bensalem serves as the ship on which I have begun a journey I never intended to make. Bensalem is not the island haven which Francis Bacon invented for his lost travellers, nor the home of peaceful investigation which Elizabeth Sewell dreamt of making for the lost students she saw and the sinking realm of education she knew. I remember that there was talk in the beginning of learning how to think, and very honestly I had never thought about thinking before. As we all were, I was required to decide the substantial questions of what I wanted to study and how to go about achieving this. My education could be viewed as a naïve mistake and a waste of time by the traditional academic world because there are certain standard requirements which I have not yet filled. It could also be seen as a groping and growing attempt to make order of the apparent chaos which I faced in the investigation of my interests and the independent organization of my course of study. Both of these observations are realistic and true because, in questioning the validity of my work at any particular time, I was forced to justify to myself the route I had chosen and to re-examine my particular goals. In developing this process of self-judgment and evaluation, and in integrating three summers of field work in Mexico with course work at Fordham University, I have neglected to fulfill ordinary requirements for a standard major field of concentration. Because everything around me was changing shape, size and position as a normal condition, I set myself and my inquiries as the only stability in my Bensalem life, mainly for the sake of my own sanity. Whatever I began in my first year I carried through to my third year and into the present (the study of Spanish and Urdu and the cultural consideration of various indigenous groups in Mexico). I worked very closely with my advisers, who never questioned my academic judgment when I presented my study alternatives and the reasons for my choices at a particular time. Our growing friendships allowed us to discuss my interests and work as well as their own at any time. These informal yet often exacting relationships formed the major part of my Bensalem academic exercise. I kept all of my advisers officially informed of my whereabouts through trimestral reports on the reading and investigating I had completed. The absence of grades or any competitive gauge and of requirements or a prescription for the proper consideration of a field of interest made it necessary to reach a realistic academic perspective on one's own work. Consequently, I often found myself asking faculty to set requirements for me, which luxury they rarely provided. I overcame the one disadvantage of having chosen a field which was unknown to our own Bensalem faculty by finding a prepared and willing mentor at Fordham.

I worked along with him in undergraduate and graduate courses and coordinated my summer field-project findings with the theoretical investigations which he required of me.

There was no plan for the particular education which I made for myself. An accidental juxtaposition of specific people, books and things have brought me to where I now stand. I look back and can scarcely believe that I have actually lived with an Otomí Indian family for four months and have taken part in initiating health and hygiene programs with the villagers and in vaccinating 1,200 children against tuberculosis, that I have lived with a small-city mestizo family and have taught English in a small neighboring colony, that I have completed a year of advanced study in Mexico City. The latter offered me a critical look at university teaching methods, and a chance to consider the nature of anthropology, as well as pedagogical alternatives for an intercultural experience geared towards directed observation of foreign cultural organization. My approach to the understanding of culture is not unrelated to the original purpose for requiring the study of Urdu of all Bensalemites: to cause us to think about our Western culture through direct exposure to an Eastern language and culture. It was a beautiful idea for Bensalem, but the Urdu requirement was dropped by the group in our first fall term.

The descriptions of my summer projects may sound very impressive, yet I am the first to admit that each of them failed. Although the specific actions were sincerely carried out, from the American vantage point it is quite obvious that in every case we acted *upon* the villagers, that the projects had not been their own. We were aggressive in our efforts to change their life-styles without first understanding what their life-styles were and without involving them in the process of change. The most frightening aspect of the projects, in retrospect, even though we can tabulate all of the "good" things we did, is the fact that we cannot begin to see the harm we might have done.

Ill-prepared, student-initiated projects play dangerously with cultural factors of which students are not fully aware. At the same time such intercultural experiences can be successful educational and global-awareness-raising experiences for the student. Thus I think there is need for serious examination of the educational potential of intercultural field work projects. A curriculum can be arranged around a program of consecutive field projects from any focus that a student chooses. He can analyze past projects and develop preparatory investigation for future ones. Third World living experience, if wisely planned and directed, may allow the interested and mature student to reflect on his own particular cultural preferences and vision, and thus bring him to awareness of the choices in his own life. It may lead him to deepen his commitment to dialogue with other cultures in order to see their particular cultural visions. American foreign policy sits in quite a different light when it affects one's own friends and adopted families.

A positive analysis of the public failure of Bensalem is a difficult assignment for any of the experimenters. The anxieties that came with taking an undefined position in an undefined environment and the frustrations of trying to introduce definition into an environment which preferred chaos as a natural state of being affected all of us so greatly that I believe we have all come out changed. The dimensions of our social chaos were so bizarre and unpredictable, growing progressively and irreparably worse from the third day of our existence, that those of us who went in looking for an educational alternative have come out with a despairing skepticism of all communal educational experiments. They all begin with the naïve hope that a group of young people will come together in a communal searching for alternatives to the present system. But we know that the presence of interested and presumably sincere persons in an unstructured space will most likely destroy rather than create any beginning for an educational experiment. The contemporary attitude that freedom of choice makes a subject matter relevant for the student is the championed precept of all educational experiments. But we know that a totally unstructured situation creates a vacuum in which the student floats blind and paralyzed with little hope for recovery unless the student moves independently to structure his or her own life. One risk of educational experiments is the cold shoulder given to the unorthodox B.A. in formal academic circles. But we know that the major risk lies in the uncertainty of personal survival amidst microcosmic societal chaos which cannot be controlled, and in the challenge of attempting a self-educating process which is personally vital and which cannot be contained by any one of the fashionable and limited concentrations offered by contemporary institutions of higher learning. This knowledge of experimental situations is purely experiential. Some observers might blame the failure on a miscalculation of some sort or on the admission of particular members to the community. Some might say that we did not work as a group to communicate and build a community or that we should have established firm criteria for either of the factions (academicians and communitarians) in order to oust one of the internal groups or simply split into two independently governing bodies. We tried various combinations of these alternatives without success; every attempt was unviable because we had no mechanism to *sustain* any of the proposed structures. The future experimenters with the Bensalem model cannot know the overpowering and self-defeating anxiety of living in such an uncontrollable environment, nor will they believe their particular endeavor susceptible to destructive chaos. For this reason I find it very difficult to explain, or merely describe, my three-year journey to anyone who has not attempted the same. It is nearly impossible to imagine oneself removed from all ties to society—to any human society—and left to one's own resources on a stormy sea to bear up against the naked elements, within and without, with thirty other such young people and a handful of faculty members.

II Antioch-Putney Graduate School of Education

. . . spinning thread-like shadows that connect memories held in palms of those you love.

ROY P. FAIRFIELD

DREAMS

From the Antioch-Putney Catalog
1971–1972

The Antioch College Master of Arts in Teaching program was originally designed to prepare secondary school social studies teachers. The program has now been broadened to include elementary education, counseling and supervision among its areas, and the master of education degree has been added. This broader program is in response to the wider interests of students and to the needs of the broad educational community we seek to serve.

We now attempt to develop educational professionals in the several areas through training designs grounded in five areas of concern. The first is to deal with particular professional abilities and attitudes. Our objective is not only to develop immediately useful skills. We also aim at attitudes appropriate to long-term successful contribution in a variety of learning situations.

The second concern is for task-oriented materials in educational psychology, sociology and politics. The educational professional must know something about human behavior in general and the psychological aspect of learning in particular.

Also he must have knowledge of contemporary educational bureaucracies and how to cope with them to achieve his own goals.

Third, educational professionals inevitably serve, and learning inevitably takes place in, a societal context. Forces outside the school, in subtle, complex and dynamic ways shape the learning environment and process. In order to deal with these forces our students must know something about contemporary problems in civil, social and economic rights and issues of race and intercultural relations. These issues naturally engage the broader fields of economics, political science, psychology, sociology, history and the humanities.

Fourth, the Antioch graduate training programs encourage individual development and responsibility, initially by placing responsibility for individual programs on the student. More than this, we seek to encourage self-awareness within a humanizing learning process. By keeping our student-faculty ratio low, we maximize the opportunity for continuous dialogue at all stages of the program. By deemphasizing grades and traditional course structures, we free the student from many of the usual undergraduate and graduate restraints, thus enabling him to come to grips with his own identity and its relationship to teaching and other educational activity in a pluralistic society.

An important aspect of student responsibility is a governing mechanism for the graduate school that permits wide and meaningful participation. While each center develops its own particular decision-making processes for program design, personnel selection and administration of the center, these processes normally include all-center or town meetings coupled with an executive committee and a personnel committee. Further, each center chooses equal student and staff representation to the Graduate Council (GRADCIL), which develops general goals, policies and directions for the graduate school.

Coordination of the academic and experiential dimensions constitutes the fifth feature of our programs. Since Arthur Morgan became president of Antioch College fifty years ago, the undergraduate work-study program has been a distinctive feature of learning at Antioch. We carry on this proven strategy by assigning each student a career-relevant work experience in conjunction with the on-going schedule of seminars, discussions and independent study. This experiential dimension is broadened further by wide and active participation in the general educational community and in the society at large. We believe that these two, the academic and the experiential, are the warp and woof of the fabric of learning.

In 1963 officials of the Putney Graduate School of Teacher Education proposed that Antioch College take over its plant and program. Antioch accepted this proposal and founded the Antioch-Putney Graduate School, developing new programs based on the work-study plan and offering a master of arts in teaching degree with concentration in the social sciences and education. While the particulars of curriculum were left to the Antioch-Putney faculty, it was agreed that each student should earn an M.A.T. degree and gain enough professional education and social science credit to obtain a teacher's certificate, preferably in the state of his choice.

The first group of ten students, recruited in June 1964, represented a cross section of American colleges and universities, as have the students since then.

Today the number of students has grown to over 200, and the program centers are located in Washington, D. C., Philadelphia, Yellow Springs, southeast Texas, and Putney, Vermont. The special stress continues to be on social science in addition to the particular professional program or degree pattern. Within the social science area, problems of civil, social and economic rights, emerging nations and peoples, and intercultural relations are of greatest concern as aspects of the traditional fields of economics, political science, sociology, history and psychology. Each center in the graduate school has its own special interests, such as rural education in Vermont or Chicano studies in Texas. Furthermore, each student's individual design makes the variety of actual degree patterns quite diverse.

Work assignments have been similarly diverse. Most students teach in elementary and secondary school and community college classrooms, but some have worked in administration, counseling, special education, supervision, curriculum development and community education.

Accompanying the expansion of program and degree designs has been an attempt to diversify further the student enrollment. Today the students are a heterogeneous mix of ethnic and radical traditions and social and economic backgrounds and come from a wide variety of colleges and universities. Unlike most teacher training and education schools we enroll more men than women. The age range is broad, primarily because of the participation of experienced teachers. A large number of Peace Corps and VISTA volunteers have entered the graduate school.

In collaboration with schools in two cities, the graduate school is trying to discover how people of the school's neighborhood can have a substantial voice in the conduct and policies of the school. We have been testing different patterns of school staffing by using neighborhood interns, graduate interns, undergraduates and sometimes high school pupils as members of the teaching group. In one of our training institutions we have brought together community school council members (elected by the people of the neighborhood), teachers, school administrators, neighborhood interns and professors to discuss and train for productive ways to improve the schools.

Antioch-Putney graduate students are responsible for their successes or failures, although supervision and guidance are provided. If one cannot handle his own responsibilities, he is advised to withdraw.

In the choice of candidates to be admitted, the graduate school will consider the extent of the student's qualifications based on the following criteria:

1. Nature of the student's interest in meeting currently pressing social and educational needs.

2. Background in the social sciences or in other academic areas.

3. Intellectual ability and habits of inquiry.

4. Strength and flexibility in interpersonal relations.

5. Resourcefulness in problem solving.

6. Sensitivity to cultural outlooks other than his own.

7. Capacity for understanding and appreciation of his own heritage and personal development.

REALITIES

From Power to Poetry?

ROY P. FAIRFIELD

Mr. Fairfield is presently coordinator of Union Graduate School, an institution to be explained in the essay that follows, but for some time served as the director of the Antioch-Putney Graduate School of Education—"coordinator" and "director" being other ways of saying "chief administrator." His essay is a fine example of the immense energy that flows through all educational experiments at one time or another, and for this reason it should be especially savored.

The Antioch-Putney Graduate School of Education was conceived in romance, delivered by forceps during a caesarean section, nourished on sweat and enthusiasm, matured through the use of every human passion, and it may well die if its members forget these poetic origins and processes and kill one another in a power struggle.

Historically and simplistically: Antioch-Putney was born of a fusion of a fourteen-year old graduate school on the side of Mt. Putney in Vermont and the imagination of several Antioch colleagues with the vision to project Antioch's work-study program into the graduate arena. By rotating groups of eighteen prospective social studies teachers through the Yellow Springs and Putney campuses and teaching situations, we hoped to utilize fully the 38-acre Putney campus and evolve a flexible program (with no grades, no fixed curriculum and few preconceived guidelines) to assist individuals in evolving self-directed lives. The initial three-member faculty enjoyed wide parameters for developing free-swinging processes; the thrust was experimental, experiential and empirical.

Since the first group entered in September 1964, to the present, we've moved from a two-campus setting to six, from ten students to two hundred, from secondary social studies to elementary and administration, from MAT program to both MAT and ME, from three faculty to fourteen plus many adjuncts and associates, from concern primarily with Appalachian education to involvement in every type of community, although most stress is on the urban, from 10 percent minority involvement to 40 to 50 percent. We've also evolved from the neat symmetry of groups of eighteen students alternating academic periods with smooth rhythm to every nameable pattern in space and time.

Here is no usual pattern of American education, no Monday-Wednesday-Friday classroom syndrome. Here is no "normal" setting of courses, since students and faculty plan the curriculum jointly. Here is no fixed pattern of relationship between student and faculty; in fact, the normal professional distance between faculty and student tends to melt away since most perceive one another as colearners. And since this is a program-in-emergence at every moment, I cannot be sure that the program I now describe will be in existence when this is read! In fact, it is not quite accurate to talk about "a program"; there are many programs in existence at any given moment, one for each emerging person in every emerging time period in a vast landscape.

I was once having breakfast in Washington with a colleague from the Philadelphia Center of Antioch-Putney and one of his students. The student was bitching because he was getting "no help from Antioch." I pointed to his faculty colleague and asked, "Who is that?" The student, a bit surprised, called his colleague by name. So I pressed, "Isn't he helping you?" The student responded, "Of course!" So I reminded him that he was from Antioch. On the plane returning from D.C. it occurred to me that this student, like so many of his friends, was "hung up" on identifying Antioch with a particular piece of geography, Yellow Springs. So I scribbled a note which has been revised from time to time and circulated among our students in an effort to get at the dimension of space-time-learning currently emerging in this country.

Where Is Antioch?

Where is Antioch? . . . Antioch-Putney? . . . Antioch-Columbia?

In Yellow Springs? at Putney? "over there" in Phillie? or out in San Francisco? or "down there" in D.C., or in Maryland? Where?

Or maybe, When is Antioch? . . . Antioch-Putney? . . . Antioch-Columbia? How? Why?

Can there be either ors if we would destroy that last parochialism of easily visible place clearly spaced in time? or space time? or what Whitehead once called the fallacy of simple location? Also, how retain that 360 degree angle of vision on every plane of space-time-psyche if abstracted from the processes of Antioch? Antioch-Putney? or Antioch-Columbia?

Antioch is:

• Students in a seminar in Putney, Yellow Springs, Columbia (Md.), Philadelphia, D.C., or in Bogota, Tubingen, London or Guanajuato.

• Students on a co-op job in Brattleboro, Berkeley or Boynton Beach.

• A faculty member reading a log or a term paper or a prospectus for independent study in a 747 over the Rockies or Omaha . . . in a hotel lobby in Chicago . . . or waiting for a train in Grand Central, in an office in Putney or Dakar . . . or going to a dentist in Columbus, an optometrist in Boston, or an internist in L.A.

• A student and a teacher sitting under the big birch in Vermont, on a park bench beside the White House, visiting a school in Harlem, talking by a winter's fire anywhere.

• Or a student-teacher in Yellow Springs, Bennington or Germantown.

• Two students sharing a room and the agonies of self discovery during an internship or ten students recounting experiences to a teacher in a cellar bar in the District (zip code 20009) or others sharing openness in a professor's study or living room or backdoor yard, talking, talking, talking.

• Or a student . . . or a teacher . . . or the president talking-walking, walking-talking, reflecting on the pregnancy of silence.

• And even teacher-student-friends and friend-teacher-students arguing vehemently over the tactics and strategy of decision making in marathon sessions which make the eyelids heavy and the arteries dilate . . . arguing the gaps between self-expectations and realization, dream formulations, the eternal chasms between ideal and achievement, hypothesis and conclusion, the chasms within the ravines and gaps within the crises of confidence and communication.

• Carving out projects, proposals and plans for working in a thousand settings from Tucson to Franconia Notch to Lagos, from Lagos to Calcutta, the Marianas or Appalachian and Hawaiian Beachheads . . . projects as extensions of flesh and blood and nerves and the heady speculations of Marshall McLuhan or what seems like the inevitable marriage of TV and the computer: computervision.

• Or talking with alumni in Chicago or Miami or New York or visiting them in Cameroon, Senegal or Bangkok.

Where is Antioch? When is it? How is it? It is *when*, it is *where* and it is *how* you look at the it. The identity of heart-mind-nerve in a process whose implications run through the finger-tips, in lightning-flash hot-lines between Putney and Stockholm, Cleveland and Guanajuato, in thunder confrontations with Mississippi sheriffs, Cincinnati judges and Washington jailers.

Just as New York is not America, neither is Yellow Springs Antioch. Our cosmic village encourages the perceptions and feelings of paradox, irony and tragedy; challenges the parody and pathos of those parochialisms which paralyze man's human-ness. Comedy, yes! tears, yes, if perspectified. And for any parti-cle in the amalgam to call atom "Adam" is to risk the fallacy of simple location in space-time-psyche and hence breed self-defeating and even self-deceiving prophesies! The whole sys-tem lights up during each brainstorm.

Where is Antioch? Antioch-Putney? Antioch-Columbia? Maybe where anybody is asking, "Where, when, why, who, how and even, ought there to be an Antioch?"

More important are the people. When that first group of ten arrived, to find three faculty members, they expected individ-ual attention, and they got it. At Yellow Springs we met in biweekly seminars, at public lectures, in the cafeteria, at organi-zational meetings to share concerns and ideas about what we would become. When we reached Putney in January 1965, we lived together under the same roof. Although we didn't have the "compleate commune," we did many things communally, plunging into a sixteen-hours-a-day "routine" of seminars, field trips, independent reading. Students engaged in housekeeping required by community living. In addition to holding seminars on educational problems and methods, we held sessions on poverty and civil rights. The dialogue was constant, whether on trips to Vermont schools, on a visit to Harlem, in the backyard or in the cellar working on a pesky water system. We watched President Johnson give his State of the Union address, sat up half the night talking about it. We worked in small groups of two and three to discuss Huxley's *Brave New World*, to weigh the Supreme Court's most recent decisions on civil liberties problems, to evaluate an article I was writing on "The Negro and Humanism." And even as Berkeley students clamored that winter for more contact with their professors, we engaged in continuing discussion about both academic and administrative matters. Students contributed significantly to purchasing books and constructing a library as well as recruiting, admissions and choosing consultants to visit the school. Early, too, they participated in budget construction and accounting.

Subsequent events and trends of the times have a way of filtering out the agony and rationalizing the dissonance. In many ways we anticipated teacher education and other kinds of graduate education by several years. But it was not easy. We knew we were in a fishbowl and had to hold the Putney beachhead for three years in order to hold the property (part of the contractual arrangements); we also knew we had to break even fiscally or have the Antioch faculty vote us out of business; we knew that we had to "prove ourselves" academically since the North Central Association would be looking at all of Antioch's credentials within four years. And as the first and second and third years rolled on, we had to find loans, internships and other sources of income for an increasingly expensive program ($1,500 in 1964; $3,750 in 1971–72). By dint of working the 25-hour-day, persistence, enlisting skilled proposal writers, we managed to manage most of those matters with as much "success" as most institutions (plus or minus 10 percent accuracy). But the people-problems, we had with us always. That is at once the agony and the ecstasy.

We had our share of both triumph and trial. We used the logging technique as a means for students to record their reading, their problems, their goals, their hurts, and the open sharing of such logs afforded faculty ample opportunity to study both the concordancy and the dissonance, the inner and the outer lives. No report will ever reflect more than a flicker of these life impulses; after all, James Joyce used many pages to express some sense of the life of one man during one day in *Ulysses*. But a few impressions may suggest:

One of our first students both ran and skiied cross country and introduced his peers to the excitements and vigors of sauna bathing, another, pressing for more student power, never let us forget Berkeley. A giant birch tree, three feet in diameter, was both a boon for our esthetic sensibilities and a bane of our collective lives when we tried to protect it from those who would peel bark, swing in the branches or hang ropes for swings (but we did have some smaller swinging birches in the lower woods where it was fun to demonstrate, especially for city folk, the wisdom of the Frost poem). The tension of completing the Major Projects (theses?) and getting them in on time, the tension of the first terminars (terminal seminars) when we were not quite clear whether we were participating in evaluation sessions or simply reporting in "one more learning matrix," the hang-ups of individuals about me as authority figure.

And it *was* difficult for me as "director" in those early days. I had taught in conventional settings at Bates, Hofstra, and Ohio University even while involved in hundreds of student bull and rap sessions, working with students maintaining the Appalachian Trail, holding open house and eating cake for nearly two decades. I had left Ohio University where my classes averaged ninety and my dreams of lecturing to auditoriums filled with automobiles became poignantly suggestive. I had left that for "classes" which would be eighteen at most. But little did I reckon with all of the implications of self-directive education, where the word "director" is a dirty one, where the role of "director" is nonfunctional, where "director" and self-directing are contradictory. So it was *not* easy for the proverbial "old dog" to learn the new tricks.

But after all, my intentions were good. So, my several years of work within self-directed education have led me, through paths of bitterness, to an increasing appreciation for the existential moment of awareness, to a profounder understanding and internalizing of paradox, irony, humor and contradiction. I've come to appreciate Jung's view that perception is 95 percent projection (a friend says that the percentage is too low). Hence, I've developed a whimsical motto for myself: "To be of use, you must take abuse." And this is no masochism; rather, it's an estimation that human beings do find it difficult to manage their own lives. They need human support without being controlled. They need to know that "somebody is there" without that somebody checking up or watching. Hence, to utilize a recent stenographical error, I've learned to view the need for psychology without spychology. And there is an irony, of course, even in preaching what one practices.

So I learned new ways to appreciate and support Antioch-Putney and later Union Graduate students. [Union Graduate School, like its undergraduate counterpart, University without Walls, is a graduate school literally without walls. Students enroll at Union for the Ph.D., but spend almost no time at Union itself. Rather, they outline their own unique program of study and are free to pursue it at any of Union's participating colleges and universities, for any amount of time at any one or all of these, usually as apprentices to particular and well-known professors in many fields, until the doctoral degree is completed.—Ed.]

I pressed students to write logs to get in touch with what is relevant to them and to help them set reference points: one student asked if he could do this in letter form, sharing his carbon copy. I said, "Fine!" He began slowly; we talked about his feelings, his view of specific books, his reactions to people. The effort broke his paralytic dam; he began to write reams, gaining writing and observational skills he didn't know he had.

In attending seminars and terminars I learned to write grooks, Piet Heim style, as a novel way to hear words, expressions and cries of "Help!" The process also enabled me to release personal tensions of boredom (I've been here forty times before!). And thanks to some training from Ben Thompson, my Antioch colleague, I learned to listen at several levels of psychological reality.

In reading logs by the cord I rarely made a declarative statement, except perhaps to suggest a book or person to see; rather, I asked questions that might lead rather than threaten; and some of those comments became central to discussions, both academic and personal.

In short, I gradually came to appreciate more of the subtleties of human support and expressed many of my own frustrations and irritations in my own log or in personal letters to old friends rather than venting them upon the perpetrators. To wit I:

Drive sixty miles over icy Vermont roads to visit a student teacher only to discover that she had left school that day without indicating where she was going. Get a phone call at 3 A.M. to hear, "I just felt like calling." Have a cook agree to do one thing and he does another, students and faculty colleagues likewise. Am cursed with every four-letter word available and still love the person. Stand by helplessly while my students are "fucked over" by a mediocre and "dying" principle or department chairman and try to figure what is best: take on the establishment or encourage the student to tell him to "fuck off."

As suggested by the "Where is Antioch?" comments, it became increasingly clear as our program reached "global" proportions that human support must be achieved through every medium of communication; also, that it had to be accomplished without much thought of geography. So I:

Met one student in New York to discuss strategies of obtaining an abortion (how fast we've bridged this space in five years!) Racked up huge telephone bills to help settle an incident in which an intern embarrassed school officials in Washington, D. C. Wrote fables to get across a point about which it seemed that we all should laugh.

For instance, once at Putney we all became so discouraged about the wretched condition of the building that I dashed off a fable in five minutes one night, shared it with a group of students sitting around the seminar room, worked with them on a few modifications, then dittoed it for general circulation. It's the story of how Antioch obtained the Putney property from a group headed by a Quaker, a man whom the community perceived as too liberal and one to whom a huge table in our living room there became symbolic:

The Old Culture House

A white-haired old man grew tired of living high in his northern-exposed, sunless and damp mountain home, growing cultures for a famous biologist. One day he decided to give his house away and move into the valley. So he walked down to the nearby river towns, crying in the streets, "House . . . for gift! House . . . for gift!" But nobody accepted his offer. They had heard of his discontent and knew he would give the old house away only if the new owner promised to raise cultures. Finally news of the offer spread to a distant spring, and a young romantic hiked seven days and nights to reach the mountain where he soon clinched the deal. After a harrowing head-long tumble the old man went far away to be with friends.

The young man soon discovered that the northern facade of his new home covered much dry rot. The rafters sagged, the sills cracked, and the paint chipped; the well was full of dead snakes and frogs. Also he learned that he had inherited a bagful of ill will from neighbors who thought the old man too well read. The young man struggled month after month to raise cultures but grew more and more aware that his own culture was being lost as he swore longer oaths each day. Seeing that both hate and fate were turning tables on him, he finally climbed to the roof of the old culture house and jumped a thousand feet down the mountainside.

Moral: You must always look a gift house in the south.

Some of my fables were more bitter than this, but we laughed and cried over them together. Too, I would share grooks, haiku and free verse with students and alumni; I always felt that some of these processes had been internalized when I went to my mailbox to discover somebody had reciprocated. A literary purist might argue against sharing such doggerel, but the students' barking responses suggested an openness. As somebody once said, everybody has fun with a pun; those who enjoy enjoy, those who criticize feel superior! I spent one evening talking about some of the following observations after a stormy meeting we'd been holding to discuss a Constitutional Convention for Antioch:

Around the table
name your name
play it sober
all the same.

Meet 'til 12
break the session
hold your guns
take the lesions

Hold your tongue
keep the face
slap his hand
holding mace

Purple skirt
panty hose
charming people
where she goes.

His face was black
guts on the floor
a beautiful buck
Why make him a whore?

We are players
in the theatre
of the absurd
throwing darts
at veins
so blue

Steer agenda   it's difficult
smoke a pipe   to tell
tempers ready   the false
with a gripe.   from true.

I also tried to get us to search into another difficult and tense
situation by writing another poem, discussing sharing; I called
it "Conference":

We sat five hours   to the beast
rapping our gums   in all of us
knowing full well   without eating
no dumb   or defeating
group were we   ourselves
trying to see   as we
relations and sets   walked
with a bet   down avenues of
we'd thread   low thornbushes
the worst of mazes   to find trust
with amazing results   in a glance
just by talking   or glean a gleam
and talking   in another's eye
and listening   or
whisper
of gently spoken word.

But all such interactions with students need not develop painfully. After two young women took my wife and me on a birthday picnic, I sent *them* a gift:

May Picnic

Sycamore shade
and more shades of the pastoral
gentle stream
kiting hawks
red-winged blackbirds
(in hollow trees)

> wittled sail poles
>
>   ("jump over the stile")
>
> a style of life:
>   relax
>   drink   talk
>   eat   laugh
>   pun
>   and run
> for whirling paper frisbees or plattersbees
>   joy
> or tell tall tales of Greece
>   Modern: Z
>   Ancient: Xerces
> watch a spider crawl across a bridge of grass
> spinning thread-like shadows
> that connect memories
> held in palms of
>   those you love.

More recently, upon receiving a very zen letter, there seemed to be only one way I could reply: the date, salutation, two poems and my signature (a colleague observed it as "perhaps the brightest thing you ever did, educationally"). Today, I attempt to spin log phrases or incidents into haiku, written along the margins or catch the spirit of the day or an image in the form of a haiku under the date at the heading of a letter or a scribbled note. My own recent discovery of haiku and the writing of haiku in split seconds between heavy minutes of involvement is joyfully shared with students in a variety of ways. At one point I wrote a five-page ditto effusion, "Haiku & You: On the Use of Haiku in Teaching the Social Studies" as a way to encourage Antioch-Putneyites to use the Japanese poetic form for honing their own students' sensitivities and senses of humor. Too, it was fun to refer them to the gift of a book of haiku sent by a Dutch friend: *Bug Haiku.*

Sharing is hardly one-way; hence I've always learned more from students than they from me. Not only have they given me insights and picnics, but also the knowledge that faith in their capacity to be creative generates more life-giving experience than the opposite viewpoint. Such faith has led to cooperation in writing articles for the *Humanist*, which I serve as associate editor. It encouraged another student to do illustrations for an article I edited for the magazine, then to spend several weeks in the editorial office feeding the staff his perceptions of our needs. Others helped me edit a book, *Humanistic Frontiers in American Education* (Prentice-Hall, 1971).

Speaking of logging, as above, reminds me of another cooperative project that was fun. A friend, Johanna Halbeisen, sat in my study one day rapping about the way in which her undergraduate work related to her Antioch-Putney experience. As we shared our thoughts about logging reactions to books, dreams, fears and loves, an idea hit me: "Say!" I exclaimed, "let's do a dialogue on logging for the conference we're having next month." We talked some more, then agreed to do it under certain conditions: I would write the first paragraph and she the last; we would write the same number of paragraphs, then splice them into a collage without any change in the order in which they came out of our respective typewriters. It was fun to do! Each of us wrote thirteen sections and had to reverse only two paragraphs (to avoid awkward repetition). At the conference we read our sections alternately. We were never quite sure about the impact of the reading, but we've duplicated and circulated it widely among students and friends in the educational world. It's too long to repeat verbatim here, but the first few paragraphs are relevant in this context:

Duo-Logue

R: Once upon a time, 1965 in fact, during the neolithic era of the Antioch-Putney Graduate School, log writing was required of all Antioch-Putney students. We said, "We don't particularly care what you say, how you say it, what form it's in, but just write. Naturally, you can turn in what you wish. We just have one requirement: you must share it with one member of the faculty, and if it is to be entirely confidential you should write on the cover of it: Not to be seen by anyone but *So & So.*" That was six academic years ago. Now, log-keeping is optional, but it is my contention that it's a valuable way to learn. In fact,

> There's somethin' about a log
> that takes you out of the fog
> those rolling sentences
> are pure repentances
> makes you feel less like a dog.

J: What is a log?—the almost-caught-it-on-paper, a file folder of papers, bits and pieces, explosions, the hate letter that was never sent, wonderings, wanderings.

R: Log-writing can include anything you do, from the very intimate to the very public. And after all, if you're doing it *for* self-catharsis, *for* developing self-motivation, *for* improving your ability to clarify, *for* the record, *for* sharpening your communication skills what does it matter that it contains only those things which you're *against!*

At Antioch-Putney we have written many community logs; that is, we've logged our program, *after the fact,* from its outset. Not only has this been important for reconstructing the program for outside observers, but at its best it has also been important for maintaining a kind of "academic openness." Except for individual conferences which, of course, maintain a person's privacy, Antioch-Putney activity has been relatively open to the scrutiny of other members of any given community (or center, such as at Philadelphia, Baltimore, Washington, Yellow Springs.) Too, this relates to the so-called administrative and governance phases. Although the very first students had a significant share in the planning and construction of the school and the processes, later generations (each generation of students in this MAT program is at most fifteen months long) have had even more to say about programs. Between 1968 and 1971, students and faculty experimented with joint governance, for individual centers, as well as the school as a whole. The mode: participatory democracy and a more functional representationalism; the object: to give every person a piece of the action. The purpose was also humanistic. *Unfortunately,* the Antioch-Putney federation (a loose system of entities tied together by common purposes and processes) did not have an Alexander Hamilton or James Madison writing their constitutional procedures; *unfortunately,* the poetry of human concerns got crushed by the determination of a few persons to play power games, hence we moved from poetry to power-seeking; *unfortunately,* many of the human gains made during the first years of the program now rattle loosely, ambiguously and precariously in a confederated context. But one must look forward with hope rather than backward with regret for (as Judy Scotnicki points out elsewhere in this book) it is a verifiable fact that there were students who grew immeasurably toward being self-directed humans during their tenure in the program.

It is difficult to say how many hundreds of hours Antioch-Putney students and faculty have argued and agonized over Antioch-Putney's mission: should we help people become better teachers? *Or* should we develop people familiar with and able to become agents of social change? Far too often, of course, the issue is stated in this dichotomous form. And, naturally, when stated in either/or rather than but/also fashion, the argument becomes polarized. Too, when students and faculty factions evolve ways to grab power, those most powerful tend to determine program direction. Tie this to racial questions and you wind up with the kind of power Donneybrook that Antioch-Putney experienced during much of 1970–71.

Students who focus on changing individuals tend to identify with the humanistic philosophies of Carl Rogers, Sidney Jourard, Abraham Maslow, as well as educators writing in the same vein. Hence, they are long on "doing their own thing" (in both the good and bad sense of the expression). They are long on directing themselves, hence resent any direction by faculty colearners. This has led to some incredible hassling, also some incidents of which any graduate school might be proud. Specific incidents:

One fellow brought his entire clique to a terminar (we sat there on the grass in Vermont, overlooking the Connecticut River, the bees and jets and roaring cars cutting through our awareness); he turned on some rock music, then read a one-page statement which said among other things, "Screw you, faculty" and "I verify myself." (That was the day he decided to take me on as "authority figure"; he and his colleagues assaulted me verbally and were stunned when I sat for two hours in that hot August sun and said nothing.) It is difficult to tell how much that incident may have related to his eventually landing in a mental institution.

A girl phoned me from Philadelphia one night and said, "Look, I'm so upset by what's happening in this center, nobody doing any work, that I'm going to see a photographer, get a picture blown up to life size, write '60 Credit Hours' on my forehead and take it to my center director and ask him to give me the degree."

One black faculty member sat in my living room before a seminar of twenty students (as guest from an urban center) and said repeatedly, "Our major task as an institution is to free the domestic third world from colonialism." That center, thoroughly converted to Marxist philosophy, began to insist that its faculty file lesson plans for the courses they were offering.

Three center directors, convinced that social purposes were more important than individual-change purposes (among other reasons), teamed up on the dean to effect his dismissal and convert the federalist organizational scheme into a confederative one (power over poetry).

Ostensibly, social change agents would "do battle" for third world minorities, other downtrodden people (even, perhaps, for children in the golden ghetto). But it's a matter of method —and outcome: are those who would adopt a Marxist (and which, Leninist? Stalinist? or humanistic?) approach, complete with ideology, humane people? Can ideology lead beyond fanaticism? If one uses violent means, can he/she harvest peaceful ends? These and other questions involving tactics and strategies of social change become the central issues in constructing learning matrices. And, of course, one might easily predict the victory of "power over poetry" among those believing in "poetry over power" since the former rarely tolerate, let alone encourage, a loyal opposition.

There have been moments of personal pathos and tragedy to mix with the human contacts, warm and mature:

One fellow is nearly killed "tooling" a motorcycle through the Putney pasture, falling off, stabbing a kidney on a sharp stick.

A Washington intern traumatized by a murder in his apartment building.

Many demoralized when individuals do not live up to their rhetoric.

Most white urban interns frightened by physical threats and violence.

Most Antioch-Putney students demoralized by the bureaucracy, mediocracy and ineffective educational system which kills kids.

A community problem when a female student "makes" a member of a minority group—the most way-out persons having difficulty with public orgasms.

A black student is upset by a faculty colleague giving him a poor letter of recommendation; the professor is upset when he learns that the student has filched a copy of the letter.

A Donneybrook occurs when three students "steal" a center's personnel files to prove how insecure the security is; meeting, threat and counterthreats, heated verbal shafts touch off irrational kindling. Younger faculty member (who knows all the revolutionary rhetoric) swings fists at student and is headlocked by another student fresh from surviving in the Vietnam jungles.

Many march on Washington with the intention of winning movement "union cards" by going to jail.

Former Peace Corpsman and faculty lose draft board battle and Corpsman is drafted with a determination to stay out of Vietnam.

Many, too many, help bring Antioch-Putney's fiscal solvency into question by refusing to pay their bills (two counterattack by taking Antioch to court when we put their bills into the hands of a collector; one writes me a "Screw you" letter defying us to get to his wallet through the Veterans' administration or even Congress, where he has many friends!).

And a girl nearly suffers a breakdown in an urban setting, drops out until she can recover equilibrium.

Another girl, during her second day of teaching, witnesses a stabbing between members of different gangs in her seventh grade; fortunately, she had been toughened to some degree for the experience by the death and blood scenes in West Africa.

This list is so thin and so shorthandish that it does little justice to the in-depth knowledge we have of the human dynamics involved in the day-to-day, month-by-month processes of Antioch-Putney. Nor will two other cases probe too much more deeply; rather, they are suggestive of the total gestalt in which we in experimental and experiential education are involved, as compared with the minimal contacts most faculty and students have in most higher education.

Every time I open one of my desk drawers, I spy a .22 caliber bullet that I "captured" (along with the gun) one night at Putney when a husband-wife team broke up, both figuratively and literally; a memory of urgent knocks on the door at two o'clock, an apartment in a shambles harboring the refugee wife, threats of killing, racing automobiles in the night, rational talk at four o'clock, reconciliation, peace by five and exhaustion with which to deal with teaching strategies, curriculum and private logs by eight o'clock the next day.

Or another tragedy: bringing a black civil rights worker from Mississippi to pick brains for a masters degree and pick apples with which to pay the bill. Four months of painful work, then bang: reversion to alcoholism. He's kicked out of his host's house, harbored in the graduate school, offered wine (by those who didn't know the story, for we'd tried to save his face). Stupor. He falls off bed, cuts face on bedrail, is rushed to hospital in ambulance. Hospital refuses to let him stay (probably because he's black): he's tied (a civil rights worker *tied!*) into bed to prevent recurrence of accident. All-night vigil by two students and a faculty colleague; he eventually winds up in mental hospital, given leave of absence from program, finally resigns;

an unpaid hospital bill continues to be a nettle in my foot.

External data suggest another kind of failure, the phenomenon of the drop-out. These come in several varieties. Some students discover that they cannot "dig" free-form education; they may come to that awareness when they face their peers and/or professors to say, "I'll do whatever you say!" thereby ceasing further attempts to be independent learners. So they drop out psychologically, perform routine tasks in both classroom teaching and seminars, get by with as little and as uninvolved work as possible, gain their degrees and prove to critical observers that Antioch-Putney works no better than State University Q. A second kind of drop-out is he or she who literally drops out because they're angry with a person or situation and cannot redirect anger creatively to face one key question: can you expect to change elementary or high school students if you're unwilling to change yourself? But the third kind is quite a different type: he or she comes to appreciate self-directed education so well that he or she asks, "Why should I bother with an Antioch-Putney degree when I can learn all I need to know by myself?" or "Why should I work hard to gain my teaching certification to become a member of the Establishment and wear myself out working in schools that are educationally bankrupt?" I've known several of the latter so successful in internalizing this "failure" that they virtually drop out of the mainstream of American society, take up candle or sandalmaking, live subsistence lives, hence are unable to pay Antioch-Putney. Is this failure or success?

Probably no teacher-education program where there is real concern about what is happening is without the nagging question of the appropriateness of their graduates in doing what they are ostensibly educated to do. Ironically or paradoxically, that group of faculty who perceive themselves as being most socially responsible may, indeed, be most irresponsible. Why? Because all too often the success of an institution is measured

by the number of its graduates placed in those jobs for which
they are aiming. Whereas, it might be argued that teacher education institutions are most successful when they find many of
their graduates *not* entering the school world! That argument
would have to take into consideration: the potential teacher's
perception of the coherence between his own life-expectations
and that which the school might ask him to do, that person's
consideration of the school in relationship to the total society,
that person's efforts to be his own man or carve out his own
identity, that person's view of "professional" expectations.
Since, typically, professional organizations, attitudes and codes
destroy individuality, enthusiasm and life itself, I believe that
the word "professional" is one of the dirtiest in the English
language. At Antioch-Putney we have had to consider the humanistic implications of these arguments, these perspectives on
"failure" and "success" in order to keep our own heads straight.

However heavy the toll of the Antioch-Putney program on
some psyches, especially those of urban interns, it has wrought
some profound changes in persons and processes. I know that
it has been "good for me," having given me ample opportunity
to practice my humanistic philosophy, express myself in a variety of forms, experiment with ideas which would have never
been possible in traditional learning settings. I believe I listen
better, write better, think better and even feel younger than I
did a decade ago. And though the program may have chewed
up some of my colleagues, because they could not stand the
heat in the kitchen, could not tolerate the ambiguities, were
unwilling to evolve philosophies that would include uncertainty, paradox, irony and humor; nevertheless, Antioch-Putney has been in the vanguard of some interesting processes that
have profound human and learning implications.

We experimented with urban internship approaches to experiential teacher education "early in the game." We had one

of the first portable videoing programs in Washington, D. C. We ran an early Teacher Corps group. Built into the procedures at the beginning was the concept that students should move in and out of at least two Antioch-Putney centers, to get some feeling for change and changing sites as a means of learning. Too, we retained the field trip from the Putney Graduate School of Teacher Education, making school visitations and Southern trips intrinsic parts of the learning matrices. Also, we eschewed the use of grades in our evaluative processes; we reasoned that the faculty certainly ought to know a person well enough to certify him, since all colearners rubbed shoulders closely. Our transcripting process is a concession to the reality that students need teacher certification, but we approach the matter from a different angle. Rather than establish courses with numbers for which students sign up, we involve them in seminars, independent study, field trips, and so on, in a whole sense. Upon completion of the year's work, we then organize a transcript and assign numbers for what they actually have done during their tenure in the program. In one sense, writing a transcript is creative writing. And one of the courses I most enjoyed verifying: Insights While Running—one quarter hour!

A persistent problem, however, relates to the fact that we evolved processes over a long period of time, that a student generation is so short and faculty members get chewed up so fast; it is a problem of effecting continuity of process. It can be argued that one is most humane if he lays down a body of rules that a person can follow with exquisite care, for the person then always knows right where he is; this is, indeed, a motive for constitutions and by-laws. But it can be argued with equal vehemence, as Jefferson reminded us, that no generation should bind the hands of another. Hence, after three or four years of operation, there was some pressure to pull our rules together to avoid the whim of faculty evaluators. And after all, we were now too large and too geographically dispersed to do it all by word of mouth. At that point I set out to outline credential procedures, course construction, the graduation process, the nature of terminars and the major project, as well as other nuts-and-bolts matters. At the close of my "Introductory Remarks" to that never-to-be-published document, I wrote:

> It was my whimsy to call it a "Footbook" rather than using other more conventional names, for it seemed to me that we wanted to preserve the notion that we could "kick around" any of the things contained therein. In short, shall we say that the processes are in a state of fluidity and that what we do can be living proof that words do not necessarily freeze.

That the "Footbook" was not "long for this world" is evidence of the ephemeral nature of such compilations, as well as testimony to the soberness of a colleague who felt it was an undignified name for a serious process (irony? paradox? humor?).

We may have established one other first in the Antioch-Putney program than that of running interference for the Adams-Morgan community school in Washington, D. C. (a first that has been amply discussed in the press, in national magazines, and in both anger and joy). That first: the use of poetry for helping student teachers and interns see themselves as they may be seen by both supervising critics and students. I've discussed this elsewhere ("New Use for the Muse?" *The Journal of Teacher Education,* vol. XX, no. 1, Spring 1969, pp. 17–22). It is enough to remark here that the capturing of impressions via metaphor during any class provides the student a dimension of the total gestalt that is virtually impossible to achieve through any other means of evaluation, video, the sociogram, systematic evaluation or wise counsel. The poetry need not be very good; for, after all, it need be shared by teacher and student only; but it does call for openness, a willingness to communicate.

The search for open communication between all colearners in the learning process has been far from universal. Some faculty and some students have sought closed spaces in order to gain sanctuary and/or retain sanity. But it has been my assumption from the outset of Antioch-Putney and from the outset of the establishment of the Union Graduate School that every form of communication, from noisy words to silent language, is important. Hence the sharing of fables, poems, questions growing out of seminars (I developed several essays in which there was not a single declarative sentence; cf. "Preface to Inquiry," an editorial in *The Humanist,* vol. XXVII, no. 1, pp. 1–2) and community newsletters or "ditto effusions," as I prefer to call them now. I've never stopped to add up the total number of pages (mostly single spaced) turned out for the purpose of keeping all members of the Antioch-Putney network informed about various happenings. These are usually titled to capture imagination at the outset (because there's nothing very exciting about a dittoed memo): "Minutes from a Yellow Clock," "A Few Chips off a Log," "Sundry from the Mundanery," "Madness, Inc.???" "The Human Comedy" (which sometimes isn't so funny). I type most of them directly onto a ditto master in order to maintain the spontaneity that Antioch-Putneyites have come to expect from all processes. A paragraph chosen rather randomly from these hundreds of pages may be suggestive (from Yellow Springs, August 11, 1968):

> Things have been happening at several levels, both internal and external, intrinsic and extrinsic. The group which came in from Putney on June 24, most of them, has been meeting once a week to discuss various problems in historical method which they thought might help them when they take up the classroom stance again in September. We've had reports and discussions on academic freedom, technical historiography, alienation, etc. Last week Barbara Cianelli, whom some of you know, tore a page out of Joyce's *Ulysses* and did some *explications de texte* very

effectively; the times seem to have caught up with Joyce, for the passages didn't seem half so radical to me on Thursday as they did 20 years ago. Incidentally, that was a red-letter day in a couple of ways. Barbara and others have been writing lyrics to well-known songs, such as "Onward ghetto teachers" and "Oh where were you? oh where were you? oh Walter Reuther where were you when they passed out those lunch tickets," etc. I'll try to get a set of the songs and send them up for the Putney bulletin board or bring them with me and sing some solos (!), to illustrate when I come up next week. I even tried my hand at it and came up with the following:

On a knoll far away
stands a school, lackaday,
the symbol of nuthin and change
(then, from the Fugs):
nuthin, nuthin, nuthin-nuthin (to be shouted at
nuthin, nuthin   the top of one's lungs!)
Dewey, nuthin
Johnson, nuthin
Nixon (less than) nuthin
How I love that old school
where the cook makes me drool
and the teachers still make me a fool
          nuthin, nuthin, nuthin-nuthin
          . . . oh well, what the hell. . . .

Get me to sing it for you if you want a laugh! Anyway, back to the story: we had fun singing the songs, then that evening (just before one rippingly violent thunder shower) we went over to the Outdoor Education Center and serenaded the Baltimore and Philadelphia interns, as well as the Putney interns. I had told the group the day before that things were too damned serious over there, and it's time that they did some laughing. I had printed up five of my fables and distributed them for the laughter mills.

Although alumni have had ample opportunity to ask me to stop writing, the feedback has been essentially positive, only one person having been asked to be dropped from the list. One of these Effusions, mailed on Lincoln's birthday, went out with a penny scotch-taped to each copy, and on St. Patrick's Day one year we stapled a piece of green ribbon to each letter. When one alumnus got into the spirit of the thing and mailed back a quarter with his letter, I thought it might prime the pump to staple a dollar bill to next year's Washington's Birthday letter. Many alumni, too, are aware that I often mail Christmas letters on Bastille and Human Rights Days. Too, we sometimes mail alumni letters with special spaces (in free-form boxes) for responding. These help counterbalance the one or two questionaires we've sent out to elicit opinion or invite alumni participation in ongoing process construction.

The paragraph from the August 11 newsletter suggests some of the unpredictable things we've done to keep humans humorous. But we've also had fun designing imaginary courses such as Crap Detecting 501 (with thanks to Hemingway), Hang-Ups 503, Advanced Goofing Off 607. Each year, too, it has been fun to demonstrate my belief that the Sears, Roebuck catalogue is a marvelous vehicle for assessing American civilization: the pages advertising bathrooms leads me to a long rap about the need for a Ph.D. thesis on "Informal Learning From Mail Order Catalogues in the Back Houses of America, 1890 to 1933," for I remember vividly that there were at least two purposes for using the Sears catalogues in my grandfather's barnyard privy in the back country of Maine 1926–1931! By sharing my fables liberally, I've induced the writing of other fables, some of which satirize my whimsy, exaggerated sense of the ridiculous and even my seriousness. But that's what makes experimental and experiential education and close learning situations both fun and insightful. Sometimes the humor route seems to be the only way to score a point. For instance, at one time I heard so many persons saying "bullshit" to anything they didn't happen to like,

I wrote a fable featuring the adventures of several fireflies eaten by a Black Angus bull that were finally "farted fecally into the family pasture," a fable with two major morals; namely, that "bullshit is not necessarily *all* bull" and that " 'bullshit!' is an alimentary linguistic nicety, of Freudian etymological derivation, which usually refers to the other guy's behavior and motivation." Printed later in *The Humanist* as an editorial (cf. "The Fireflies and the Bull: An Anatomy of Bullshit," vol. XXX, no. 2, March–April 1970, pp. 4–5), it created sufficient stink among both students and magazine readers to have made it a joy to write.

One major consequence of my involvement in the Antioch-Putney and Union Graduate programs: deeper insights into human problems and personality. Hence, on a sabbatical year's leave (I was determined to have twelve months "free" for at least once in my life, so I did more during that goof-off year than any year previously), I read a thousand pages of mine and other Antioch-Putney log materials, read them at virtually one gulp (the best way to get sense of self movement and change). Hence I relived some of my deep involvement in other people's lives. Suddenly I asked myself: why not an up-dating of Edgar Lee Master's *Spoon River Anthology*, this one to focus upon students' dying self-concepts. So I worked a month or so on forty sketches, comprising a prose view of forty persons alongside a free verse statement which each of the people ostensibly uttered. Here is one of the shorter samples:

Nola Katz

My assumption was clear:
she had survived in a
barrio in Caracas, surely
when she came to intern
with us she could hold

I felt "the urge to kill"
or will away a promise
I could not keep
because he pushed me
into corners

herself together in an
urban classroom. She had
taught while in the Peace
Corps, would teaching in
the ghetto be so terribly
different? But none of us
counted on the rise of
black power. No white
was *necessarily* welcome
in the ghetto? Nor did we
count on her indecision,
her struggle with pastor
father over the nature of
"mission." If she had spent
more time doing, she
might have evolved the
being she fantasized and
shed her impotence. But it
isn't easy to bridge the
gap from Pasternak to
Claude Browne, nor can it
be done gracefully when
you may have to look into
forty-two seventh grade
black faces every morning
and wish you were dead.
Before and during her
interning I pushed her too
hard, expected her to
come up with answers,
verbal answers, however
tentative they might be.

They could become the
shoals for her to grasp no
matter how hard the sea
was pounding. Also, I saw
pushing itself as a shoal, a
"thing" to make her angry
when her blander self
might wash away. But

I would not escape.
He seemed to want
to extort
confession
of conversion
from simple Christian
view
to all the intricacies
of existentialism.
I felt "soft" toward him
at distance
and admitted with friends
his brain was old
and his body young
though he was really fifty,
but "close up" he
threatened
the hell out of me
with those hard questions
I wanted to slip
in my ragged search
for new identity.
But like the lobster
in his newly taken shell
I miss the self
which I once wore so well.

when she quit cold at
Christmas and joined our
study seminar, I slipped to
silence, feeling that she
needed healing and hardly
further wounding. That
silence was deafening at
her farewell.

Another fact of life for those working in experimental programs: usually they *are* born of romance, hence the originators find themselves doing everything from teaching (in a broad sense) to administrative work to janitoring. The day is twenty-five hours long. And sooner or later, before the institution is large enough to differentiate functions (by which time it probably is not too experimental), faculty members find themselves head over heels into admissions work if they haven't stumbled onto that activity even before the first student shows up on the premises. During the early days of Antioch-Putney we literally beat the bushes for students, hence reading application forms was more a matter of curiosity or an opportunity to peal foreign stamps off Peace Corps volunteers' applications than a vital function. True, we did it conscientiously, but we were inclined to take anybody who was warm; in fact, we had open admissions, and Antioch-Putney students were well aware of this reality. In later years students themselves have been deeply involved in reading folders, interviewing prospective students, gaining perspective on their own perspectives through involvement in a process that is all too often done unfeelingly. Only recently, after spending an evening with some twenty Union Graduate School admissions folders, did I conclude the evening by trying to catch the poignancy of my own feeling in a poem entitled "Admissions Committee Work"

I
browsed
all too lightly

through that score of lives
catching a ball of fire
bare-handed
almost too hot to handle
touching a sensitive spot there
almost hearing the "Ouch!"
sensing some pathology
in the pit of stomach
as
tho
I had lived the trauma
to the hilt
enough to wilt
the strongest stalk
smelling the putrid sweat
of foundry and filling station
work experiences
and tasting the bitterness
of black and female hostility
little ability to laugh
lying on sharp needles
too pointed to prick thin skin. . . .

Ours has been a process of involvement and immersion (cf. my chapter, "Teacher Education: A New Immersion!" in a book I've edited, *Humanistic Frontiers in American Education*. Englewood Cliffs, Prentice-Hall, 1971, pp. 75–83). Even where the results have been most disastrous, the framework of intent has been essentially humanistic. Both students and faculty have for the most part caught the spirit and the excitement of experimentation. Even the crassest faculty and student Machiavellians (self-defined and self-styled) would argue that they were trying to improve social conditions, were working toward a particular form of social justice. But I am convinced that we have not worked hard enough thinking through and articulating some fundamental paradoxes; nor have we wrestled enough to design ways to face such paradoxes; nor have we yet, as Americans, faced the reality that there may be paradoxes and ironies which are as much like "givens" as the force of gravity. To wit:

It is my considered judgment that experimental education in which there is the *promise* of individual support and individual attention to individual problems creates an exponential rise in expectation concerning interpersonal relationships between faculty and students. Yet, the increase in energy level of any given colearner is at best arithmetical. And even if faculty members are doubled and tripled in number, the net effect is still arithmetical or geometrical, hardly exponential. Such rise in expectation and the resulting gap between expectation and realization is bound to create unpredictable anxieties and alienation. That faculty member who intends to remain in this kind of education had best plan some blue sky for himself (vacations, siestas, spontaneous flower-smelling and star-counting), or he'll get chewed up in the system. We need more personal testimonies and log exposures to help us understand this phenomenon. We need to expand the blue sky test that I occasionally give deans (How many haiku have you written today? When did you have your siesta yesterday? Are you willing to talk about the goofing off you did last Monday and that you project for tomorrow?) We need ways to check the Sense of Humor Quotient (SHQ) of prospective faculty and students so that they can with a certain glee cut open any stuffed shirt they encounter, to let *all* the straw and sawdust trickle out!

Other paradoxes we need to explore:

That the closer one is to the center of power, the less power he has to achieve humanistic objectives.

That the less visible he is by Madison Avenue standards, the greater the possibility he has of achieving humanistic goals.

That the more he talks and writes, without listening, the less he'll communicate (let's see, was it Jung or Freud who said that one must learn to hear with his eyes and see with his ears?).

That the more he attempts to achieve status and human understanding concurrently, the greater the possibility of failure.

And, too, without being masochistic at all, wise faculty and student colearners will recognize that to be of use to their fellow man/woman, they must take abuse in conventional terms. Too, these wise colearners (and it's obvious, by definition, that my students and I fall into this category) will learn to see disjunctive and dissonant situations and even accept some of them as givens, insusceptible to the correction most Americans try to impose when they appoint a committee to solve the difficult immediately and the impossible a little later. Too, to two other tunes: those colearners will realize that even they often fight to make the world safe for hypocrisy and that they may wish to join Schopenhauer in chanting, "Give us this day our daily illusion." Or, if they are a bit more existential, they can go forth more positively each day to face an enchanting (as well as mixed-up) world, reassuring themselves with "Give us this day our daily surprise." Antioch-Putney people, like parents and those engaged in other human development enterprises, may have to face another paradox: their greatest task is to put themselves out of business.

The phone rang from Florida at midnight: Dean Lowman thanking me for existing. I asked, "Why that effusion?" He said, "Because I just spent the evening with a long-held hero, Sidney Jourard, and he treated me as an equal." "So you've been generating dignity," I observed. "Say, that's a good way to put it," he remarked. "O.K.," I promised, "I'll send you a poem about it." "Great!" he exclaimed, "and remember that I'm from Farmer City."

So after our fifteen-minute conversation, I wrote:

Escape from Farmer City

> Sit not
> at the feet
> of giants
> like galley slave
> pulling an oar
> with blindness
>
> but balance
> on teeters
> taking him up and down
> with your thoughts
> and joy
> generate dignity
> two thirds man
> one third boy

Since joining the Antioch-Putney program in 1964, I've heard many students agonize, complaining because a communications gap opened a credibility gap in their people-trust. And it seems they do not hear or do not understand when someone reminds them of Joyce's effort to delineate the many pregnant levels of living and consciousness. Obviously, there is no one way to cope with so complex a problem, save perhaps to value the process of coping, a process perhaps all too evident from above. I have increased confidence in the process of open-ended, free-formed, self-directed learning. I feel an increased confidence and security in the power of a metaphor, whether precise or rich with suggestion. And I agree with my dear friend and colleague, Ben Thompson, a founder of Antioch-Putney, that programs such as Antioch-Putney, Union Graduate School and University Without Walls test the assumption that freedom *can* work.

The Paralysis of Selfcil

JUDY SCOTNICKI

Judy Scotnicki, whose essay follows and who has recently completed
her degree at Antioch-Putney, worked closely with Mr. Fairfield during her time there. Presently she is working in the Washington, D. C.
area.

**Anyone who rides Antioch-Putney rides the meanest
horse around, probably the meanest thing on this
planet.**

**Antioch-Putney is possibly the freest graduate insti-
tution of teacher education in the country.**

During my tenure in Antioch-Putney from the fall of 1969 until
the winter of 1970, I experienced some of the meanest and
freest learning of my life. If engagement is a form of creativity,
it was a highly creative period for me.

To give you a flavor of what I lived, I have to take you and
myself back there, knowing that some of what I perceived and
felt will be representative of the experiences of others who

were in the program at that time, and some of it will be unique to me. To complicate the narration—it's all history now.

I believe that just about everyone who came to Antioch-Putney Yellow Springs in June or September of 1969 came from traditional undergraduate backgrounds. There was very little in our formal education biographies to prepare us for the free approach to learning, that is designing our own programs, whether independent study or seminar configuration. Consequently, at our first "orientation-registration" meeting we were "roadrunner style" signing tentative course sheets for seminars, projecting even into the spring of 1970.

Most of us hadn't started our teaching internships yet. We were still rooted in group study, legitimized by a faculty person as being the prescription for authentic learning. There was quite a response for the thought-to-be "safe" seminar. I think the prevalent attitude was that we wouldn't have to do most of the work ourselves. The faculty member leading the seminar would give us a bibliography and suggest topics for reading, discussion and/or writing.

Several people got a jolt when at one of our first seminars (about one-third of the center was there for the first session) the faculty person told us *we* were supposed to decide what we wanted to do in his course. A syllabus and bibliography sort of cushioned the blow, but those essential props were missing at the second seminar in American history, also held that evening where the same faculty person blithely announced there wasn't a bibliography—it was all to come from the group. It's no exaggeration to say that it took another meeting of three hours of hassling to come up with a half-hearted, nonetheless desperate, "O.K., Roy, order a few readings from the Heath series *Problems in American Civilization*," although we dutifully put to a vote which particular lessons in the series we wanted for common reading.

What's significant about this initial difficulty and real cop-out

in group designing of a seminar is that the phenomenon repeated itself each quarter, except when the faculty person assumed responsibility for the direction and content of the seminars. Incidentally, last summer when my fellow students were
polled as to where they saw the greatest need for improvement
in the Yellow Springs program, can you guess? "The seminar,"
said a majority of those responding to the evaluative ques-
tionaire. Since not many of us thought in terms of paradoxes, I
don't think we were bothered by that one any more than we
were by several others: we were drawn to Antioch-Putney to
avoid a structured curriculum and prescribed behaviors in
managing the affairs of our graduate school, yet were proverbi-
ally trying to structure our seminars and governances; we
wanted freedom to "do our own thing," but we consistently
demonstrated inability to cope with that freedom; we wanted
power, but we didn't know what to do with it when we had it;
we demanded openness at meetings, but shouted "bullshit!" or
cut a person off when he tried to relate his feelings to the larger
group; we were a very uncommunicative society; still, we referred to ourselves collectively as the Yellow Springs community.

I know our communications problems in Yellow Springs were
shared by the other three Centers of Antioch-Putney (Philadelphia, Putney and Washington, D. C.); and when all the centers'
representatives came together, it was hell on four wheels. Fortunately, it was only on a quarterly basis that the four centers
convened for GRADCIL. The graduate council, the governing
body of Antioch-Putney graduate school of education, alias
GRADCIL, brought itself into existence in 1968. Composed of
faculty and student representatives from each center, it was
supposed to make major policy decisions that affected the running of Antioch-Putney as an institution. By the time I entered
the program in 1969, GRADCIL had the reputation of being
unable to agree on anything but possibly the hour of adjourn-

ment. It lived up to its reputation in my tenure in Antioch-Putney, too. GRADCIL's big project in 1969–70 was a Dean hunt, since the acting Dean was resigning in June '70. After six months of debating the notion of having a Dean, GRADCIL came up with four nominees (two student-suggested and two faculty-proposed). Each center was to work out its own arrangements for interviewing the candidates, giving reactions in writing to the delegates to the February '70 GRADCIL where votes were to be tallied and a new Dean to emerge.

I had the unforgettable experience of going to that GRAD-CIL, listening to around seven hours of people screaming at each other on Saturday—it was like watching people play hand ball off each other's heads. Sunday morning everybody must have had a "people hangover." Late Sunday, following caucusing between and among individuals and centers, several straw votes and several "official" votes, one candidate crossed the finish line. But a hitch developed because he was not everyone's favorite (just the favorite of a simple majority), hence GRAD-CIL balked at declaring him the winner, deciding at this late date, "We need another process."

Well, if not a Dean, how about a Dean team? This was facetiously called DEANCIL by an observer—one of the few light moments of the day . . . the weekend! Another alternative seriously discussed was a proposal to bring all the four candidates together and let them decide who should be Dean. This motion was modified and finally adopted: to bring the top two Dean candidates together with the acting Dean, representatives of students and faculty from each center and President Dixon of Antioch College and let them come up with a selective process. As a postscript, "ADHOC-CIL" (minus the two leading candidates) decided that GRADCIL had in fact selected a Dean, even if it didn't recognize itself as having done so!

Now if this GRADCIL business is confusing and/or mind-blowing to read about, imagine what it was to live through! GRADCIL had this hang-up, call it unwillingness or inability to make decisions about anything consequential. Question: can we reason from this general malady to particulars? For example, did the individual centers and individual people have this problem with decision-making? Right on!

In our Yellow Springs All-Center monthly meetings (in theory all faculty and students; in practice any from the center who were there) during the fall of '69 and early winter of '70, the easiest decisions were those made concerning who would be on committees. We had two major committees: the Yellow Springs Council or YECIL, supposedly the policy maker, and the Personnel Committee, charged with interviewing and hiring faculty. As long as the committees didn't do much, nobody complained or asked definitively at the all-center meetings what these smaller groups were up to. Then when it became known that YECIL was giving out money for student projects (the source was our tuition money, legitimate according to our own center governances) and that the Personnel Committee hired faculty for the winter quarter (also legitimate), heads began to come out of tortoise shells—"What are *they* doing with my money?" "How come *they* hired a guy at $800 to teach a course nobody is going to take?" Notice how we turn on our own; the students and faculty on those committees become a suspect "they", even though they were delegated by the larger group to make decisions about money allocations and faculty hiring. Before long at all-center meetings we were questioning, item by item, a committee's action, undoing but rarely redoing its work. At our February all-center meeting, a peeved chairman of that group said, "Maybe while there is still time the Yellow Springs Council should vote the all-center meetings out of existence!" We had a sense of humor about ourselves until, I guess, the Kent State murders.

On May 5, the Yellow Springs Center's facility was shut down because of its location on the Antioch campus with the rest of the college on strike. Well, some people got excited about this unilateral decision by the center director (chief administrator, coordinator of the center's activities). So via a phone chain, the students called an all-center meeting for that evening:

Act I

Scene 1.   The setting: a small classroom in one of the buildings that was open on campus. The players: full-time faculty members, including the center directors and maybe a third of the students enrolled in the Yellow Springs center. The action: one faculty member pounding his desk saying he's going to offer a "methods" seminar that's *really* useful (he's been holding a methods seminar the whole quarter). A student is yelling he is going to lead a course on Marxist analysis of capitalism, first meeting to take place at the same time one of our full-time faculty (also at this meeting) has his normally scheduled Marx seminar. In this din another student is making a motion to give a $500 donation to the Black Panthers' Defense Fund. Some of the players not talking or protesting are simply voting on everything that's happening. Then we're reminded that we're late for the mass Antioch community meeting. The curtain falls on minds and bodies scrambling for the door.

Scene 2.   The same evening. A few people—three Antioch-Putney students from another center—who felt railroaded by that meeting, which they asserted was "irrational and a bunch of bullshit," decide to take counteraction to match the irrationality of the meeting in which they just participated and thus bring everyone to their senses. The three manage to get into the Antioch-Putney Yellow Springs facility that houses our student files and remove them from the building.

Act II

Scene 1. Next day (May 6). The three antagonists issue a memo to the community telling us of their caper and assuring us that our files will be returned for the ransom price of a "sane all-center meeting."

Scene 2. Telephone chain in full swing as the SOS goes out for the center to come together. Allegedly, one faculty member even drove to Dayton to make sure our students in that area not only made the meeting but were sufficiently enraged that sanity would be precluded.

Scene 3. The meeting. Our center meeting room is packed, more people than have ever attended an all-center meeting in the three quarters I've been at the center. The three antagonists are present, but the protagonists aren't too interested in what they have to say unless it pertains to the location and repossession of our student files. Suddenly, a motion is on the floor to call the police (very seriously proposed). Before it can get a second, one person gets the floor and starts trying to put the antagonists' act in perspective, his part reminiscent of the Greek chorus's role in tragedy or comedy, but he is drowned out by the volcanic rumblings of "Get the files, and then we'll talk." The three antagonists, perceiving the script is a different one from what they had rehearsed, announce they will go for the files. Then one of them shouts tauntingly, "Go ahead, call the police." Somebody else clips, "Stop being a goddamn martyr." With that, one of our intern supervisors leaps from his position on the floor in an assault on the g.d. martyr. Before blood could be drawn, the fight is stopped and all the players decide to break until the files arrive. End of my two act play.

Insanity, tragedy, comedy—or just another paradox? We were supposedly unconcerned about grades, credits, or the trappings that have traditionally hung up graduate students;

yet, we were ready to punch a person out or send him to jail because our records were temporarily not in the office. I felt sorry for all of us that night. We lost some good people—people who had tried to be reflective and active in group processes but were now fed up. "I'm just going to finish up my work and get out," they told me.

In the following months as chairwoman of the personnel committee in the spring and summer quarters and chairwoman of the all-center meeting in the spring, I twice went through the process of searching for a Yellow Springs Center director, spending more than eighty hours in interviewing and meetings. I was called an "elitist bastard," dangerous, paranoid leader of a fiendish conspiracy to undermine the center, a white liberal, a co-opted enemy of the people, and so forth.

Just what terrible thing was I doing that was perceived to be so threatening? I was verbally urging the construction of a faculty and staff for the Yellow Springs center with a composition of people who could work with each other as well as the students. By the end of the spring quarter of 1970, one half of the staff wasn't speaking to the other half, and students were being influenced to take a particular side. Most of the students resented being put in such a bind and recognized that this state of affairs was counterproductive to all of our goals. But those of us willing to put ourselves on the line against such nonsense were in a minority. Practically all of these students were involved in finishing up their work and as they put it, "I do want to graduate and _____ might not sign my verification sheet if I challenge what he's doing." Verification sheets were pretty crucial since they were the only 'official' record of the work we had done until we were awarded our degree by the faculty and entitled to the completed transcript. These verification sheets are descriptions of what a student did in a particular course, substantiated by the signature of the faculty person with whom he has worked on the course and that of the center director.

I was in the unique position of not having to depend on the signatures of the people the cautious students thought might do the zapping because I was not finishing in the program until December '70. They were all due to finish either June or August '70. The controversial issue of late spring and most of the summer was the selection of a center director for Yellow Springs. I did not feel "forced" to support a particular favorite son candidate who had been part of the divisive element in the Yellow Springs center during '69 and '70. Although white, he managed to turn the selection of a center director into an alleged black-white conflict, insinuating that those not voting for him were anti-black. There I was after a successful ten-month teaching internship in an inner city adult education program (where I was the only white person in the organization) getting top billing as a member of the "racist" faction in the center. It's sad the way some people use the issue of color so recklessly for their own personal advancement. As I said in the beginning, I had some of my meanest learning experiences in Antioch Putney.

Favorite son did win, ending up with a full-time faculty staff of four who had more trouble working together than the previous staff. Although the personnel committee had renewed all four contracts for the next year, the center director announced in the spring that after June he wouldn't be needing the services of two of the three cofaculty, predictably the two he hadn't found compatible.

All in all, 1970 was even worse for Yellow Springs' growth in group functioning. Instead of dealing with evolving processes for managing the center and its relationships to the other centers, students aided by some of the Antioch-Putney Yellow Springs faculty just wiped processes out or let them fall into disuse. GRADCIL was dissolved by the centers' representatives in 1971. YECIL met once, I think, in the fall of 1970. The personnel committee, more or less lame duck after the summer, hired faculty, most of whom were initially recommended by the center director. All-center meetings were infrequent. Finally, the center just agreed in the spring of 1970 to hand the power over to the center director where, as one of the participants at that meeting expressed it, "the power had always been anyway."

I don't know that the dissolution of GRADCIL was a bad thing, or that allowing YECIL and the personnel committee painless deaths was a bad thing. What I view with sorrow and concern is the centralization of decision-making in the center director's hands, also that this act was as much willed by the students as by the center director. Ironically, these students began the program with the opportunity to stretch their imaginations in creating alternative social and political relationships, but they opted for the paternalistic model.

Maybe our cumulative miseducation was so thorough that our imaginations atrophied long before we got to Antioch-Putney. You may have noticed in my treatment of that year and a half as a student in Yellow Springs, and the past six months as distant observer of that scene, I've used the personal pronoun "we" more than "I." I never functioned there in an interpersonal vacuum, so it's impossible to refer to my experiences without including others. Much of my discussion has focused on what happened to the people I worked and played with when we came together as a group because it was in these situations that I had my most significant learning. For the insights I developed from participating in all-center meetings, I paid the price of cynicism. I'm almost convinced that "pure democracy" is only possible when there are no more than two people involved. I also believe that the communications problems of Antioch-Putney Yellow Springs in '69, '70 and '71 were based on lack of trust more than lack of understanding. We were not very good listeners. And when we did listen, it was just to those who reinforced what we wanted to hear.

And I'm bitter about the way the color issue was manipulated to hurt both black and white students. Last summer we were sometimes actually on the verge of genuine sharing and growth together. Then we would go to an all-center meeting where the risk of some of us really reaching out to others would be so threatening to certain people present that one of the latter would jump on a devisive tactic, usually race, because that was a way of insuring that people would not have to relate as individuals. This strategy of dividing the group into convenient black and white categories usually was very successful at preempting honest interaction. You couldn't tell people they were being exploited by "the Man" in their own backyard because they couldn't see or admit that "the Man" was some of themselves. The majority of the students in Antioch-Putney Yellow Springs in the 1970–71 group were black, and a few of them made no bones about telling the "honkies" they were going to have their way. Right or wrong, brother, it was at last going to be raw Black Power!

Still more so within the latter group than the one I started with in 1969, there was one subject we could and did ritualistically pledge allegiance to unanimously, and that was CHANGE —social, political and more specifically, change in the public school system. But what came through so clearly was that very few people were willing to change themselves. Here we arrive at perhaps the super-paradox of our "freest graduate institution of teacher education in the country." Everybody was for change as long as it was either to take place outside of themselves, or inner change if it was only something minor like trying "good" teaching materials in the classroom. Yes, some of us did read and did get excited about the thoughts of Holt, Dennison, Kohl, Rogers, et al. But too many of us were unable to internalize these writers' underlying premise: one has to test the idea of change toward his own growth in order to facilitate others in that process.

I put myself through some hellish testing, although I admit I went into some of it blind. Starting out fairly naïvely about Antioch-Putney people and the program, I was thrilled at the prospect of designing my own agenda for graduate study, teaching at the same time and sharing in the governing of my graduate school. I felt as though I was being presented with some great gift; I never had to work so hard in my life psychologically to earn such a "gift." Only after going through four quarters of the "what should we do?" seminars did I fully appreciate and intensively utilize the opportunity to construct the independent studies of my last quarter—and oh, the beauty of just arguing against myself and consulting with a cosigning faculty member. But what made the independent studies so valuable to me was that chronologically they came after I had taught and gone to seminars—I knew what I wanted for myself at that point.

I think I also outgrew ego-tripping somewhere in the dialectic of those howling, lonely Antioch-Putney Yellow Springs confrontations and my independent studies. Ego-trippers are not just afraid of other people—they're really running scared from themselves. I grew in relationship to myself, learning not to panic in my dreams nor be afraid of trying to understand what the dreams told me about myself. I coped with the waves of anxiety that smacked me when I was awake. I learned in one-to-another relationships to give of my ideas and emotions without feeling threatened or that I had to parenthesize myself out of existence.

My teaching style went through a "March Revolution." At the onset of my internship I was doing too much of the talking and almost all of the initiating of what was to be learned. It was relatively easy to get the students to take over the talking end of the relationship, but the initiating of the learning they wanted for themselves we never fully pulled off. The students felt that I should provide the materials—text or media sources —in, for example, language arts, and then advise them individually as to which area they *needed* to work in the most. What evolved was a compromise. I did provide the materials and the consulting, but I asked that they choose not what they thought they needed to know but what they were most *interested* in learning about. Sometimes they simply didn't seem to know, or what they wanted to learn was so overwhelming that they didn't know where to start. I always guided and structured more than I felt comfortable with. My criterion wasn't my 'model' mental construct of the ideal learning situation but rather one in which my students could live and develop. With each of the three distinct groups of students I worked with, I had three different classroom situations not only because of the quarter turnover but because what I learned from the preceding group I incorporated into the next.

My relationships with former students were not regulated by the quarter system; we continued caring and communicating with each other after the courses had ended. One student even wrote a letter sometime after she had left the program. As an evaluative document of my internship, it means more to me than anything my intern supervisor wrote or could have written. My student wrote to me not to fulfill any requirement but simply to express her friendship. In this letter she kerneled what I hope was my style as a teacher and learner, in both my internship and my related Antioch-Putney activities. One of her sentences says it all: "I'll always remember you as a person who tries to help, not mere mentioning of it but really, really tries." So often as teachers, as human beings it's quite impossible to measure out accomplishments, but we can weigh the extent of our efforts.

I really tried to help, whether it was in holding a center together or assisting one of my students in learning to read. And the whole thing might have been so different. I might never have known how much I was capable of if I hadn't believed that I had the support of Antioch-Putney Yellow Springs in my internship or if I hadn't had the Antioch-Putney ideological backdrop: namely, the freedom to develop myself according to my own design, not a preconceived design of the department, faculty advisor or institution. Yet I wouldn't argue that my growth in Antioch-Putney was programmatically guaranteed, or, least of all, that it was institutionally effected.

An institution denotes established, organized functions. I don't think Antioch-Putney has ever acted particularly established or organized. I perceive Antioch-Putney as a series of relationships between students and faculty and the people in the school systems with whom they worked—relationships that are very local, transient and personal. Every four or five quarters there's a turnover in students and sometimes in part of a center's administrative and faculty staff. That partially explains the great difficulties the four centers had in reaching any major so-called institutional decisions. The closest thing to an institution in our frame of reference was the center. I've repeatedly referred to Antioch-Putney Yellow Springs. Someone at one of the other three centers would probably do the same thing, maybe not even bother with the qualifier Antioch-Putney.

I think it's more accurate to talk about the directions the centers seem to be moving in, hence, the "institution." I see each center in varying degrees caught up in a parochialism, one that has already brought about the dissolution of GRADCIL. Originally, the centers were to have a catalytic and open emigration-immigration effect on each other. The idea was that people would spend at least a quarter in some center other than the "parent" center. I think this inter-center movement is of real value, but it's not practiced or in fact encouraged much these days.

Along with the parochialism, there is a reverse racism in full swing: Washington being 98 percent black, Yellow Springs and Philadelphia moving fast in that direction, leaving Putney—liking it or not—as the white center. Antioch-Putney will not be a viable instrument for influencing improvement in the American public school system if it is dominated by one type or color of student or if its vision is narrowed to what is possible within the context of the four centers' reach.

If Antioch-Putney ever "got it together," more centers could and should evolve; however, the old and new ones will thrive only with a healthy mix of students and faculty—a mesh of age, sex, color and background. This also means that students in the graduate program should come from not only recent undergraduate work in colleges and universities but also from the pool of teachers who have spent some time in the public schools. If teachers already involved in public schools were part of each center's program every year, it might enhance a center's survival capacity within a school system, as well as offer a greater possibility for center students to serve as "change agents." What I see happening now in certain Antioch-Putney centers is just an emphasizing of the "easy" aspects of the degree. As an illustration, I cite an advertisement recently carried in several newspapers and periodicals highlighting the Antioch-Putney Masters of Arts in Teaching program as one with NO GRADES, NO THESIS. This ad prompted a sign to appear in the Antioch-Putney Placement office: FLY BY NIGHT GRADUATE SCHOOL . . . $4,000 or 20,000 BOX TOPS!

I think when a journey through Antioch-Putney has come to 20,000 box tops, it's time for some radical thinking and action, not just on the part of those running the four centers but also from former faculty, graduates and drop-outs as well. Or was Antioch-Putney always a farce, and I the one who was duped?

III Franconia College

. . . it is hard, very hard, to find a place to be human in, to find people to be human with. Humanness in all its weakness and strength, humanness with its kaleidoscopic mixture of openness and selfishness, warmth and fear.

RICHARD R. RUOPP
JOHN JEROME

DREAMS
From the Franconia College Catalog
1964

The following is taken from a publication entitled, *Franconia College Proceedings: Community Progress Report,* dated spring of 1964. In terms of most college catalogs, this one is unique, as a good many experimental college catalogs are, because of its mellow conversational tone and its reticence to pin the college down to anything more than a few operational guidelines. Read sympathetically, such catalog prose can suggest many "between-the-lines" perceptions about its college that conventional catalog prose about conventional colleges seems always to destroy with painstaking explicitness.

The Value of Our Environment

When you stand on the front porch of the college on a clear day, your eye travels out across Easton Valley and up to Kinsman, Cannon, Franconia Notch and finally Lafayette which, if you are in condition, you can climb in a day. Or you can walk in the college's 200 acres of forest which serve as a laboratory for those students interested in ecology, geology, mountain climatology, natural history, forestry and conservation.

There is a challenge in the climate and terrain: the sharp air, the mountains; both demand liveliness of spirit. This trust is held for students to come, many of whom will encounter here the mountains and forests for the first time.

We want Franconia students to know how many ways values can be found in this kind of environment: an afternoon walk near the college or a full weekend trip into the deep woods; the exhilaration of a difficult climb on the high peaks or the thoughts which come while sitting on a tumbled-down stone wall; the skill and teamwork needed for guiding a canoe down a stream swollen by the spring thaw or the solitude of skipping flat stones across a still pond in the evening; the friendship of the warming hut in winter or the quiet of ski-touring down back roads. This, too, is part of education.

The North Country is also known as a place where great ideas and individualism have sprung tenaciously from a rocky soil. Though seldom immediate, there comes always a confrontation with the North Country spirit—a rich distillation, perhaps, of the New England Yankee. For students bred in these parts, it means slowly becoming aware of a style of life they had taken for granted: laconic but warm. For students from the "outside" it means the slow process of learning to communicate with people who seem to consider you even more foreign than you consider them, the slow surprise at shared feelings, the discovery of the spark within the flint.

Often the process of this growing awareness causes changes of attitudes—sometimes permanent, sometimes not. Six months has not been too short a time to see the city-bred student defending the North Country spirit against the complaints of the student living five miles away. In short, we feel there is a special value in living in an area which, more than most places in the country, has a definite personality that seems to grow out of the weather, the countryside and the character of the people.

The main building itself . . . looms over the valley and is dominated by the surrounding peaks. It is a building built for a hotel and yet a building with immense riches for imaginative development into a college. Inside are study rooms, dormitory rooms and places where students gather to talk; for the library, a cluster of small, book-filled rooms; other rooms, used for classes by day, at night places for the solitary student studying for an exam or writing a paper; art workshops and music rooms, map rooms and the museum; and the room where skis are left. The first phase of Franconia College to operate in the black is the busy, student-organized, student-run coffee shop!

Whatever, the building is—at times, frankly, a headache, at times an adventurous old ship fending off the north-country winter storms, at times a hive of intellectual adventure—whatever it is, it shelters us and gives us a home and mood for the kind of college we think we should have.

The Value of Ideals

We accept Aristotle's assumption that "All men, by nature, desire to know." We seek students who hunger for questions and answers and then more questions.

In a technological age we affirm our humanity. We believe that students too are human beings—individuals not to be rigidly categorized, conditioned, molded with preconceptions or turned into nonquestioning robots. Students are to be valued more as growing beings—unique and precious—than as precisely describable objects.

We value, therefore, an education that encourages growth into full humanity rather than mere aging. We seek to outgrow simple conformity and easy revolt.

Our ideal is a creative environment: a place where ideas are encouraged, where new metaphors come naturally, where—if it is valuable to do so—molds can be broken.

Beyond this, we also believe that there are perennial values that transcend individual men and the span of individual gener-

ations. Qualities such as honor, truth, charity, integrity, courage
and loyalty seem to be woven like golden threads in the affairs
of men throughout history.

Though these values cannot be learned in the way we usually
think of learning things at college and though adults seem to
have as much trouble with values as young people do, still we
assert that education does have to do with values. Perhaps this
is one meaning of Whitehead's dictum that the "essence of
education is that it be religious."

We would sum up the relationship of values to education as
the obligation each man has to investigate, to understand and
to act. These are the components of a decision and thus they are
central to our Core Course and to the four principles of the
college which continue to guide us:

1. It can be said, "God has nothing to fear from truth." Though
    perceived in many ways, named by many names, Ultimate
    Reality must be, for each individual, the focus of concerned
    investigation.
2. A person should seek to know himself well enough to sense
    how his attitudes, values, ideas, physiology and total person-
    ality shape his decisions.
3. Similarly, a person should seek to understand the forces
    which influence decisions of others. A man should have a
    sense of concern and respect for his neighbor, whether he
    is of like mind or living in an entirely different culture.
4. Finally, we recognize that what seems to come last in the
    process—the courage to act—is not really last at all. For in
    life as it is lived, all the other virtues spring from courage.
    The individual must learn to judge and assume the risk of
    action.

Halfway through our first year, how have we fared with these
rather lofty ideals? It has been a struggle requiring all our

strength and all our commitment, but it is clear to us that there is value in ideals. Our goals and principles serve as a standard against which we test our daily decisions and our progress month by month.

It is clear as well that high ideals do not simplify the task of building a college. Just putting together a college would have been a far simpler task than constructing a college community based on principles, many of which seem all too obscure in today's world.

Students manifest our ideals when they say that a certain kind of life is beginning for them. As one of them put it when we were studying the *Old Testament* concept of "covenant": "Beginnings and covenants are very difficult. They go from something known to something relatively unknown. Making a commitment to an ideal, an institution, a person—this is a covenant. Coming to Franconia College is making a beginning: wanting to come here and accepting the principles of the college is making a covenant."

The Value of Decisions: The Core

Visitors are not here long before asking "just what is this 'core' course?" We can explain it best by outlining the three reasons it is called "core."

1. It is the core of every student's program for two years. It constitutes almost half of his total curriculum.
2. Over the two years we study in depth twelve samples—we bore down into twelve "cores"—of crucial human experience. We choose twelve moments rich in meaning, from the distant past to the present. We search for the heart of those moments by not restricting our tools to those of any single discipline. It is not a course in History, Literature, Philosophy, Science, Psychology, Religion or Art, but it

makes use of all of these and is taught by men and women who have been trained in one or more of these fields.

3. In every case we focus on the thing which is at the core of our own lives: decision. The twelve moments are moments when someone made a very significant decision from which we can learn. By looking hard and honestly at the material, we find that the meaning of decisions becomes ever more complex; we avoid any pat formulas that explain why people decide things or when they decide, or even sometimes whether they make a decision at all.

For example, last fall we started with the moment when Socrates drank the hemlock: an exact moment which is clear and exciting. But this moment, we soon saw, is only the focus of a most complex pattern of forces, ideas and personalities which existed before and after the event. These needed to be studied. We had to try to come as close as we could to the words of Socrates, and to read what Plato and other people tell of him. Not only that. We needed to discover from Homer, Aeschylus, Sophocles, Thucydides and the visual arts the progression of values and events which led to the condemnation of Socrates by a jury of Athenian citizens who bore him little ill-will. We met four times a week for six weeks on this unit. We learned that there is no simple answer to "what was Socrates' real decision?" Indeed we ended with more questions than answers.

To take an example from the end of the course, we plan to consider Truman's decision to drop the atomic bomb on Hiroshima. What was the state of the Second World War? What were the advances in modern physics leading to the development of the bomb? How much was known about the influence of radiation on living cells? What were the historical events leading to Japan's social and political attitudes at that time? What do we know of the personality and character of Truman, the Commander-in-Chief who was responsible for the final decisions? What are the ethical and religious issues?

We value this integrated general education course as the central manifestation of our commitment to a liberal arts education: the study befitting free men. We still argue whether the goal of a free man's studies is *doing* or *knowing*. Do we seek learning to apply immediately to our own decision making, or do we seek knowledge and understanding for its own sake?

The core has contributed to a sense of community. It is a common enterprise for everyone, faculty and students, and provides a common intellectual language. It happens outside the classroom or lecture hall. Disputes and discussions continue into the night or into the countryside. A student who had never heard of Socrates is heard pounding a table, arguing about piety; a student is heard mulling over the motivations of Dostoevsky's "Grand Inquisitor"; a student wins a heated debate on the premise that original writings of ancient Greece are precious "because they are there"; these are glimpses of the atmosphere we encourage in Franconia College. The wide diversity of training and interest in the entire community enriches the undertaking: the common pursuit keeps us together as a community.

Finally, the core, like any good college course, is designed to increase—for students and faculty alike—power in those intellectual disciplines which open the door to knowledge and understanding: reading, speaking and writing. We read closely texts of merit. In groups we constantly test and improve our ability to speak in a reasoned and persuasive fashion. Since writing is one of the best ways we have of knowing our thoughts and feelings well enough to understand them fully and test them critically, the student is asked to write an essay each week. Our attempts to communicate with others are seldom successful until we can communicate with ourselves.

Productive Tension

Our academic community has taken direction from struggle with the following paradoxes and dualities:

1. We are creating a two-year college but not a junior college.
2. We serve the local community but are a private, self-governed college.
3. We base our curriculum on the principles of liberal arts and build it around an integrated humanities course, yet include vocational programs as an integral part.
4. We affirm the necessity to confront the religious dimension but insist on complete freedom of inquiry.
5. A close student-faculty relationship holds the community together; yet we do not mistake the teacher for a buddy or pal. The different roles of teacher and student enforce a real and sometimes painful distinction.
6. We go along with the traditional shape of an education: the student first builds a broad base of competence in various areas and then narrows in upon a field of greater specialization. We also know from experience the value of the opposite shape: letting a student who has a zealous commitment to one small area, if he is truly serious, really dig in and lose himself in it. If he explores truly and is taught well, he later comes to enquire with his own curiosity in areas that formerly he would have studied only grudgingly and unproductively. The core is required for both years, but otherwise a student picks his courses with complete freedom. Naturally, students are constantly urged to examine the implications of their choices by their academic advisors.
7. Finally, it is fair to say that our ultimate goal is growth, and that we believe growth comes out of freedom. Yet this does not mean the absence of limits in community life. True freedom exists only within definable limits.

REALITIES

Death in a Small College

RICHARD R. RUOPP and JOHN JEROME

Richard R. Ruopp was the second president of Franconia College for three years. John Jerome was director of public information.

The Prologue

A week after we had resigned from Franconia College in the spring of 1968, we sat down on a porch next to a stream and wrote about what had happened in Franconia College, what it meant to us.

Except for this prologue and an epilogue at the end, we have left the story as we wrote it.

Understand, Franconia College was and is unimportant the way importance is often counted. That is, "statistically insignificant." Less than two percent of the student population in the United States is enrolled in colleges with 600 or fewer registrations. Franconia is only one of hundreds of those small colleges.

But statistical significance is not the point. What happened at Franconia had to do with love and death. In the spring of 1968 many cried at Franconia. They cried because it is hard, very hard to find a place to be human in, to find people to be human with. Humanness in all its weakness and strength, humanness with its kaleidoscopic mixture of openness and selfishness, warmth and fear. If concern for tenderness and warmth and honesty seems laughable to a world grown cold protecting its vitals, then our questions are to that world. And Franconia College grappled with those questions.

It's a hard story to tell because Franconia was a place of movement—and to stop it in words is to take something away that is essential to its value.

We have purposely tried to avoid making any villains or heroes (although we were tempted because we were hurt). And we want to make clear that we wish the Franconia College of 1971—72 well. It now has a young (24) president. He is energetic and able. The board of trustees is almost completely new, one with a different vision more consonant with the reality of present-day students and faculty. New buildings have been built. In June of 1971 the last class involved in this story graduated. And times themselves have changed. This story, then, is not meant to detract from the Franconia of this year or next. It is history, one version of history, that we believe should be told. We hope Franconia will continue to live and flourish. At the same time we know it will not be the same.

We offer the following, therefore, as an unresolved morality play.

The Play

Dramatis Personae: Voice I
Voice II
Voice III
Chorus

These voices include students, faculty, administration, townspeople, trustees, newspaper reporters, members of the larger academic community, alumni, parents, police, government officials and spectators. The authors have made no attempt to identify which constituencies belong to which voices; sometimes those things are never quite clear. The chorus consists of published opinion and verifiable fact.

Voice I

The more pessimistic—and more mobile—members of the college community consider that Franconia College died at 10:00 A.M. on Tuesday, April 2, 1968.

Voice II

Our concern is to promote the spirit of intellectual adventure and to forward the academic life which has been initiated and carried forward at our college. We look forward to what now has become a most realistic promise for the future, namely . . .

Chorus

Drugs, Liquor, Sex "Rampant" on Campus
BARE "DEBAUCHERY" AT FRANCONIA COLLEGE

FRANCONIA, April 5—"A wonderful dream which turned into a terrible nightmare."

This is a townsman's characterization of an institution of "higher learning" which is making a mockery of education—a school whose birth was the pride of this White Mountain community but now has become an arena for scenes of increfiable [sic] debauchery.

College policy allows virtually unlimited license to students and faculty alike—in the pursuit of both academic studies and personal pleasures. Drugs, alcohol and sex are among the main ingredients of campus life.

Residents of Franconia, Sugar Hill, Littleton and other nearby communities surrounding the campus of Franconia College vividly describe the. . . . (*Manchester Union-Leader*, Manchester, N.H., April 5, 1968.)

Voice III

It is the policy of the college not to interfere in the personal lives of its members. The law is between the individual and the state.

Voice I

"Isn't that something? This cat and his chick are making love, and a state trooper walks in and busts them for 'lewd and lascivious behavior.' And at that moment, some other cat is over in Vietnam flying a bomber, dropping hot napalm lunches on kids, and they give him a medal for it. *That's* lewd and lascivious behavior!"

Voice III

The second president said, "The college may not have died last Tuesday. I hope not. Time and work will determine that. But the tender connections of a fragile community were strained and, for some, shattered—not by trustee brutality, but by their fear of a truly humane style. And the tragedy is that they could have had what they wanted for the asking, if they could have been gentle-voiced."

Voice I

Franconia Village is a small New Hampshire town of some 500 souls located just three miles from the granite walls of Franconia Notch, wherein stands the Great Stone Face of Nathaniel Hawthorne's story. The town was established in 1764; it would like to believe itself as rock-ribbed and conservative as New England mythology will allow.

In 1963 Franconia got a junior college. With new colleges springing up in this country at a rate of one a week to absorb World War II's baby boom, the infant Franconia College looked like an automatic success. It was the only college in New Hampshire's "North Country"—the 5,000 square miles that constitute the uppermost tip of that triangular state. And as it had acquired a huge, four-story white elephant of a summer resort hotel up on a hill above town, plus 200 acres of woodland and golf course for a campus, it began life with a fairly small mortgage in terms of conventional academic endeavors.

The junior college grew from eighty-three students and ten teachers during its first year to a full four-year B.A.-granting college with 349 students and forty-two teachers in its fifth year —1967–68. It was one of twenty-six "colleges" in New Hampshire, of which only eighteen grant B.A. or higher degrees. It also grew, primarily because of outright good fortune with personnel, into a far-out, faculty-run hotbed of innovative education, which attracted, as any new antiestablishment endeavor will, a sizeable gathering of far-out, experimental people, both as students and as faculty. Beards and long hair began to drift down the hill into the tiny village of Franconia, upsetting the tourist traders who depended on down-country dollars. Here and there, if you listened quietly in the years from 1963 to 1968, you could hear the quiet *pop* signifying that another staunch

New England elder had just had his mind blown. And when there's not much else to do—as there isn't in Franconia—gossip is no longer a luxury, but a necessity.

In addition to the social trauma the college seemed destined to inflict on its townsmen, Franconia College found its financial footing difficult to secure. Living off tuition is a nice dream, but it makes for high tuition, low faculty salaries and no "profit" for capital improvements or even much major maintenance. Particularly with a student-teacher ratio of eight to one. Furthermore, fund-raising—for an unorthodox place which valued freedom more than it valued façade—proved difficult. The carry-forward deficit grew, in five years, to $280,000 (although more than half of that was spent in capital improvements). The budget balanced in fiscal year '66–'67, but the mortgage still stood close to $300,000 in April of 1968. With an annual budget of $1.1 million, the mortgage and the annual deficit weren't shocking when compared to most of the large, stable institutions of higher education; for a small, new college with no alumni and an unfavorable local image, it was courting disaster.

Despite this bleak financial picture, the college met with considerable success in the world of academics. State accreditation was granted in March 1965, for its two-year, lower division A.A. degree. In the spring of the same year, the federal government approved the college for federal funds. The fall of '66 saw the state accrediting committee return for a careful review of the Oxford-style upper division program leading to the B.A. This program was recommended to the state legislature and approved for a four-year period beginning in February 1967. The same month, *Newsweek* picked Franconia as one of the five new colleges in the country most deserving of success, and then refunded the cost of a full-page fund-raising ad that began, "A small New England college seeks funds to remain small . . ." Franconia students who transferred out to larger institutions with broader faculties had little trouble establishing the validity of their relatively unorthodox academic credits. In educational circles Franconia College was generally accepted, often encouraged, sometimes even honored.

Voice II

"In a report of a two-month probe conducted inside the college by an investigator not in the employ of this newspaper, it is stated that the college's existence can no longer be justified on moral grounds. It is at present doing more harm than good to the majority of students. . . ."

Chorus

". . . The attention drawn to irresponsible student behavior at Franconia College has tended to obscure the positive accomplishments of the college in other respects—notably the vitality of the educational program. This from the start has been one of the strongest features of Franconia College, and it is worth noting that there has never been dissent on this point among trustees, faculty, students and those who know the college well."—from a statement issued April 8, 1968, by the chairman, New Hampshire Coordinating Board of Advanced Education and Accreditation.

Voice II

I agree with everything you say. This is a dirty business. But our backs are to the wall. Some of you may say that a bloody mouth can still swear. That may be what you want to decide. But you have to realize that's what you'll be deciding. Because they will simply close you down.

Voice III

The second president of the college came to Franconia in August 1963. Half the time he was to be minister of the local protestant church and the other half, teacher in the humanities core course at Franconia, which was to open the following month as a two-year institution. He was thirty.

The year before he had worked at a therapeutic half-way house called the Spring Lake Ranch in Cuttingsville, Vermont, while on leave from the Antioch College Extramural Department. At Spring Lake he had learned the astounding fact that we are all sick, but that we can help each other.

When he said "learned," he meant in the Jobian sense of learn: "I had heard of thee with the hearing of my ear, but I had not seen thee." And that it is astounding is sad, reflecting how conditioned his own upbringing had been by the romantic American dream: the perfect ending for the perfect hero, who has no past, does not question his future and relies wholly on his established ability to outdraw his weak and impoverished opponents.

Franconia College had no real prospect of survival. The board of trustees, all but one of them local, envisioned a coat-and-tie-for-supper junior college that would produce a ready supply of ladies and gentlemen. This vision might have been reasonable except that the first president hired a Brandeis graduate student in psychology as the first dean—who proceeded to hire a young faculty (average age 29) from places like Goddard, Brandeis, M.I.T., Harvard, Pratt, Reed and Antioch—a dean interested in educational reform first and administration *qua* administration practically not at all.

The first president was a lawyer with one year of educational administrative experience. He *wanted* to be a college president and had marvelous, somewhat frenetic dreams of educating the

souls of the young. He had been found by the business mana-
ger/vice-president, who had come directly into college administration from the optical business.

Later we found out that not only was the endowment a mea-
ger $70,000 but that we started the first year with an operating
budget $13,000 in the red with forty fewer students than an-
ticipated. And this in a town which is a pot-pourri of uncon-
nected social circles, ranging from traditional New England to
nouveau riche Swiss ski-chalet owners—a town of quiet alcoholism, at least one suicide a year and an element of Peytonplace-
ness.

Voice II

Let me say in your personal interest, if the college is liqui-
dated, your claims for salaries for the remainder of your contracts will go into the pool with the other $400,000 worth of
creditors, mostly parents, et cetera. If we go into bankruptcy,
it will be a long mess. Now let's talk about long-term funds. . . .

Voice III

There was a certain delightful naïvete in the air the first three
or four months after the college opened. The students were
exceptionally tractable (testing indicated a high tolerance for
failure; most of them were old hands at it). The faculty was
idiosyncractic, intense, full of the notion that the future of the
college was in our hands. No one seriously attempted to per-
suade us otherwise. Core took on the shape of an interdisciplinary humanities course for all freshmen and sophomores,
taught by most of the faculty, focused on decision making. It
started with Socrates and went on to Buddha, Christ, Galileo,
Roger Williams, Darwin, Marx, Freud, Marilyn Monroe and
Camus in the first two-year sequence. Under the soft-handed

guidance of its first chairman—a Williams and Oxford graduate who had taught in the M.I.T. freshman humanities program—core became a common intellectual ground infecting all aspects of the community's life.

"With my undergraduate background of literature and history and graduate work in theology and the philosophy of religion, I found core an exciting teaching experience. Particularly appealing was the notion that the 'disciplines' were arbitrary traditional vantage points from which to view the raw stuff of human experience."

Socially, things were smooth that entire first year. A girl was found on the boys' floor of the dormitory one night. There was a case of breaking-and-entering, a few incidents of excessive drinking. There were no drugs, no demonstrations, no student power. Some wished for more activity and less apathy. A community government structure was developed—town-meeting style encounter with faculty-engendered liberal rhetoric as a primary agenda. The major issue of the year was whether or not students could have cars. The vote was *yes*. One wonders at a distance if this was not the first step on the road to hell.

Voice I

Those townspeople would be so happy if we'd just have panty raids and beer busts up here and maybe roar around in loud convertibles. They want Jack Oakie and Shirley Temple attending this college, not people.

Chorus

"Rampant promiscuity is encouraged. There is no adult supervision in the dorms. Boys and girls are allowed to room side by side in some dormitories, and no one prevents them from living together in the same room. . . . Naked and drugged or drunken men and women have been seen running through the halls at night and orgies and nude parties have occurred. . . ."—From "a report of a two-month probe inside the college," as quoted by the *Manchester Union-Leader,* April 5, 1968.

Voice II

At the executive committee meeting of the board of trustees in March of 1968, the first indications of disenchantment with the second president came to light. One board member voiced the opinion that the president was a dangerous man. A letter from a student was passed around—very anticollege and antipresident. Another board member indicated that he'd checked with a faculty member, and the student was regarded as an unreliable source. A committee was suggested, to check into allegations about the president's competency, so that if evidence was found supporting them, the president could be confronted and the truth sought out.

The next meeting was of the full board, on March 8. Photostated documents—summaries of meetings held with selected faculty members concerning the president and internal affairs at the school—were passed out. Later, the board was presented letters between bankers about conditions at Franconia, a thirteen-page letter from a faculty member, copies of student publications, a copy of a reappraisal inspection report from four members of the board of a bank which held part of the college's mortgages, and a memo to the board from the faculty indicating a strong vote of confidence for the president. In all, several allegations were made concerning the president; he was not present to answer them. Some time after midnight, the board voted ten to one, with one abstention, not to renew the president's contract, which would expire June 30. It was moved to reconsider the vote and adjourn until the next morning, and the board did so.

The next morning, in the face of an increasing realization that the outside pressures from the insurance companies and banks were absolute and unalterable, the board decided unanimously not to reappoint the president under the terms of his existing contract. The president was informed of this decision. The trustees also voted to form a committee to review faculty contracts. The board adjourned until March 28.

Chorus

". . . Some institutions have had considerable success with minimum formal restraints, or none at all (re: sex and drugs); others have failed entirely with rigorous controls and penalties. The approach adopted at Franconia, which was characteristic of the college's educational as well as social philosophy, was that in matters of personal behavior the students themselves should judge their own conduct; regulations regarding intervisitation and such matters were accordingly left to the students and eventually abolished, the only rule being that the rights and the privacy of each student be respected. . . ."—From the statement by the chairman, New Hampshire Coordinating Board for Advanced Education and Accreditation.

Voice I

We started the 1967–68 academic year with several things firmly established. Franconia was generally a faculty-and-student-run college with a board of trustees who traditionally left academic and social policy strictly alone. It had more students than it bargained for: 348, instead of the desired 325. It had four crisis-filled years under its belt, one lone B.A. graduate and immediate prospects of about 40 more who had made it through most of an upper division academic program that was called a "little graduate school" for its rigor and for its predilection for delegating responsibility.

The other thing that Franconia College had that was so worthwhile was simple honesty. No double standard. We called it a lot of other things and erected a lot of self-deluding banners over it: individual freedom, the right not to conform, up the establishment. But in the end it all boiled down to an effort to say what we were, rather than to be what we said we were. Yes, we had drugs. And because we knew it was pointless to try to legislate morality, as a community we tried to deal with problems about drugs with concern: by caring. We had sex. And we knew that artificial segregation of the sexes, dormitory rules, restrictive policies were only going to push sex underground, where it had much more chance of being destructive. So we dumped the problem back on the individual. If you check into a hotel, you get a room and a room key, and your life is your own affair, whether you are seventeen or seventy. Law is between you and the state; there's hardly any point in a college erecting stricter laws than the laws of the land and spending energy trying to enforce them.

We also had beards, long hair, bare feet, strange dress styles, pets, failures in housekeeping, noise in the dorms, and squabbles with the townspeople. We had an open campus, and that gave problems—from visiting acid-heads looking for action, to visiting dogs from the village looking for romps. Our attempts to deal with these "problems" were sometimes ineffectual but were always open and honest. We were often capricious, but never arbitrary, secretive or manifestly unjust. We were terribly idealistic: we dreamed that we would never have to hide or sneak or dissimulate. We didn't want to erect "respectable" façades in front of humanness and then feel guilty about it. Unfortunately, the town, the state, the banks, the insurance companies and the board of trustees insisted that we must.

Came the deluge. In the fall, a group of students and faculty took part in an antidraft demonstration in Manchester, which developed into a minor melee. When pressed for a statement concerning the arrests of students in this demonstration, the college issued a standard blurb full of the "neither-condone-nor-condemn," "individual-acts-of-conscience," "spirit-of-free-inquiry" kind of phrases. The archconservative *Manchester Union-Leader*—a newspaper later to distinguish itself with acts of courage like an editorial blasting Martin Luther King, Jr. for anti-Americanism in the week following his funeral—accused the president of the college of "moral neutralism." Newspaper sales soared locally. And anticollege sentiment in the local village began to crystallize, nay, petrify.

A five-year master plan for the physical development of the college brought the board of trustees to a new level of interest and involvement in February. At the same meeting an administrative report was made about attempts to satisfy the requirements for physical improvements to the college property laid down by the insurance companies' engineer. And two students fielded questions about twenty-four-hour intervisitation and other concerns the trustees had voiced about student culture.

Winter is a harsh time in northern New Hampshire. Long nights, muffled sounds, reduced mobility. We had a couple of -45 degree nights in early 1968, and one spell of over 120 hours of below-zero weather. It's a good time for quiet academic pursuits—there's certainly little else to do. But with the thaws, the victims of the winter's paralysis begin to realize just how bad cabin fever can get. The New Hampshire State Police celebrated the break-up of the winter ice with a predawn raid on the Franconia campus on March 5. The governor of the state had called a conference on drugs; it was exam week; the president's contract was being discussed. We should have been able to predict the raid.

Seven students were arrested for possession of narcotics. Charges of gross lewd and lascivious behavior were also filed against three of the students plus one other person. "Lewd and lascivious" in New Hampshire ordinarily means extramarital sex. In one of the college cases it consisted of a male student being found asleep on a pile of pillows, attired in dungarees, in a girl's room at 6:00 A.M. The girl, also charged, was asleep in her own bed, across the room, in a nightgown; she'd been ill and had asked the boy to stay with her in case she needed help.

Voice III

That first year at Franconia, back in 1963, was not what you'd call a piece of cake as far as faculty and administration were concerned. Covert pressures were beginning to be brought to bear on the first president and dean to tone down "excessive expressions of freedom" among the faculty—which were undoubtedly being construed as infectious to the young in the college's charge. The dean in turn became weary from the intensive seven-day-a-week schedule spent trying to keep the board and the business manager off faculty backs, and in turn trying to keep the faculty from splintering into factions. Administrative work lagged, which in turn caused the faculty to become increasingly irritated with the administration. At the end of April 1964, the teaching faculty met for the first time without a member of the administration present. Two weeks later the first president put the dean on a terminal leave of absence without consulting his teachers.

"A horrified faculty spent two days deciding whether or not to resign and thus close down the school. Responsibility to our students kept us going. In a divvy-up of the dean's job, I became dean of faculty, and the assistant dean of students moved up to that deanship. The first president retreated to his *Reader's Digest* and his office in the face of faculty outrage. There were several fiscal and recruitment problems.

"The first president didn't resign until December, at which time I became dean and acting president. At that point some board members quit—they were, needless to say, of a conservative persuasion. The search for a new president went on slowly. I didn't want the job—I preferred being dean—but was advised by an ex-president of Wellesley that although my sentiments concerning the impossible task of being president might be correct, if the 'wrong' president were chosen, being dean would not mean very much.

"One of the men who was a casual candidate for the job, a Unitarian minister, told me, 'You become president, and I'll become chairman of the board and help.'"

On May 11, 1965, at thirty-two years of age, he became the second president of Franconia College. And the Unitarian minister became chairman of the board which lost confidence in the second president in March of 1968.

Voice 1

I'm sure the insurance companies' legitimate sphere of concern is the technical considerations of fire loss. I can see their concern with cigarette butts in the halls. But do they really think that changing presidents is going to change the cigarette smoking?

Chorus

". . . as to culpability in the present police actions, it is clear that the police did in no way communicate nor cooperate with the president and the administration, and we feel that in light of this fact, if guilt is to be assigned, it must be to the community as a whole, for one of the inherent principles of Franconia as an experimental institution has been that the community is the

responsible body, with the administration serving a largely organizational and executive function. . . ."—Letter from upper
division students to the board of trustees, March 9, 1968.

Voice I

The mood at the school, as the board met to consider the
president's contract, was foul. The faculty had recommended a
new three-year contract; the board had not responded. Many
aspects of the narcotics raid seemed to indicate an inside in-
former: police went directly to specific rooms with specific war-
rants for specific people, without consulting college records or
notifying college officials (in one case they went to the wrong
room, according to college records, and found the right person
—named in their warrant—therein.) And the timing of the raid
was such that the board was meeting as the maximum publicity
glare was just taking effect on the local village.

Adding pungency to campus gossip was the fact that two or
three members of the board of trustees had been meeting pri-
vately, sometimes with the college lawyer present, in grand-
jury style, in a motel room in a nearby town, calling in for
interview some of the faculty who had written letters to the
board concerning the presidency, some who hadn't and some
students. (The president had encouraged the community to
communicate with the board regarding his reappointment,
whatever their opinions, as early as the previous October.)

A few refused to go to such meetings. One of the college's
firmest traditions was the open meeting. Only sessions of personal counseling and "executive sessions"—wherein a deliber-
ating body was dealing substantively with individual personnel
matters—were closed. There had always been a lot of talk at the
college about "encounter" and "confrontation"; the community ideal was that you deal openly and honorably with the

people with whom you worked, played and politicked. Now the board was not only holding closed meetings with community members, as one report had it they were swearing their interviewees to secrecy, not only concerning the meetings themselves but even about their location. No tactic could have been better devised to set teeth on edge. Secrecy, of course, was nonexistent; no pledge to external trustees was as strong as the implied pledge to the community, in the first place, and more important, the tone of the secret meetings seemed to indicate an actual threat to the safety and stability of the community. It was seen as behavior "grossly destructive to the community," to use a phrase that appeared frequently in community government by-laws.

The winter term ended on March 13, and many faculty members scattered on vacation. No decisions had been reached yet, officially, about the presidency. The board was seeking further advice.

Voice II

There is no deviation from the unanimous opinion of the board that this college is outstanding in its academic achievements, and there is no sign that the board has anything but high respect . . . and full trust in faculty responsibility to shape the curriculum and devise and execute . . . teaching methods which they themselves best understand. But we have before us, and we will have to discuss it at this point, a very real possibility that the college may have to be closed. We of the board have faced up to the very grave hazards that a closing would bring to us. We do not relish this, and we propose to seek, right now, and after this meeting, for ways to carry forward. Now I think it is fair to say that the chief problem which confronts the college is in the realm of finance. . . .

Voice III

His vision of education was mediated by his educational experience:

"What I remember from grade school is little. Shooting out street lights. Stealing hub-caps in a suburb north of Chicago. Smoking a full pack of Luckies with a friend in a closet. Being the smallest kid in my class. All these stand out as more real than anything that went on in the classroom.

"Prep school was a bit different. I remember the German teacher I had for three and one-half years, because he never gave an A, was tough and distant, but when I got to Germany years later I could do more than order eggs and ask for the men's room. I remember with sardonic relish the English teacher who failed an essay I wrote in 1944, contending that Truman would win the election. (I remembered this particularly in November of 1967, when, flying to Washington, Mr. Dewey took the last seat on the shuttle next to me and proceeded to read a strategy paper from the Republican National Committee's Ray Bliss.)

"There was a history teacher who threw me out of class for a minor disturbance. He loved his material so much that I majored in history in college because I found another who had the same intense love and who worked to make the process of teaching convey that love.

"Then there was a shop teacher, young and buddy-buddy. One night he told one of my student heroes, who had been thrown out of Governor Dunmer Academy, that he should see a psychiatrist. Gordie knocked him down, and they both left school at the same time.

"I remember best from prep school the English teacher, also a coach, who married a lovely young girl named June, who gave out the mail and about whom we used to sing "June is bustin' out all over," for obvious reasons. I had boyish, Oedipal dislike for June's husband, until both of them befriended me. I graduated an indifferent student, deeply pained because as a sixteen-year-old prepubescent senior I didn't have a girlfriend."

Voice I

Let me give you an example. A freshman the year the college opened. His home was Mt. Vernon, New York. His parents were probably Jewish, I don't know. He certainly seemed to know well what being brought up in affluence meant. Teachers who worked with him here at Franconia the first couple of years didn't think much of him as a student, although he was very friendly. The mind behind the smile was dull, never having been sharpened on any problem worthy of much energy. He graduated, barely, with a "standard" A.A. degree, and we thought he'd be back off to a country club lifeguardsmanship for the summer. He went to VISTA instead.

He worked with the Navajo outside of Gallup, New Mexico, and came back honed. He worked on a thesis about the history and current operations of the Bureau of Indian Affairs, using what he had learned in his critique. The thesis was solid, not brilliant, and grammar and spelling took work, but he had by then learned about finding a good editor. He had to rewrite several parts of it for his examining committee, and then he passed a comprehensive exam in public administration and was awarded Franconia College's first B.A. He's in Colombia now in the Peace Corps. No one remembers that he was from affluent Mt. Vernon without looking it up.

Voice III

"My first two years of college were a different story: I went to an experimental, unaccredited junior college for fifteen men in Pasadena, California, operating under the unlikely name of Pasadena Branch of Telluride Association (PBTA). It became defunct shortly after I left. The parent organization, Telluride Association at Cornell University, and a cousin, Deep Springs College in California, still live.

"At PBTA there was only one administrator-teacher—a Quaker political scientist, nondirective and unobtrusively concerned. We students hacked out curriculum, went out and found teachers from Cal Tech, UCLA, USC, Temple and other nearby institutions of higher learning. We did the dishes, had a work program modeled after Antioch College's, had classes at night. People painted, danced to Prokofieff's *Scythian Suite,* wrote poetry, sculpted, fenced, climbed up Mt. Whitney and down Grand Canyon, talked politics to Leo Tolstoy's sister, Charles Collingwood, Robert Ryan. We made small public speeches, stayed up all night, drank Vermouth, dated the town girls. We probably would have smoked grass, but it was 1950.

"My academic work I do remember. Art history was exciting. When we went to see Orozco's *Prometheus Unbound* at Pomona College, I got so fired up I actually did a piece of hard research on Orozco (then Sequieros and Rivera), got my first A and set the stage for immense appreciation of Orozco's mural at Dartmouth College, which I saw some fourteen years later.

"I took my first comparative religion course and became tremendously excited that an exclusive view of Christianity as the only true path to salvation (which I had always found repugnant to my semisecularized soul) was nationalistic, and hardly in line with the view of the Christ of the Gospels. I found Buddhism, Hinduism and Islam equally heady and looked for the philosopher's stone which would indicate the great synthesis of all truth, so that later, when I read Symmachus ("The roads to truth are many, but the truth is one.") I brought some substance to it.

"Philosophy was almost my undoing. We used Russell's *His-*

tory of Western Philosophy, plus a collection of original readings under the tutelage of a young teacher who in retrospect
probably had designed the course to approximate what he
would like to have taken in graduate school. It was a struggle
I lost and didn't want to lose, but the teacher lost, too, and I
hope he learned more than we did.

"I held my first two jobs and spent what I earned as fast as I
earned it.

"I read all of Huxley's novels in a two-week period."

Voice I

Another student climbed into the drug bag up to his ears:
desire for insight. The spring of his freshman year he took a
leave of absence to live in the woods, read Tolkien from cover
to cover and explore his own mind with various chemical aids.
He had planned to ask for credit retroactively, but what might
have been worthy of credit couldn't be put on paper. He was
one of the framers of the second Community Government Constitution, the opening statement of which was "work hard and
be kind." And he did. I think the words were his.

His parents were terribly worried about him, about the college. They are German stock, and they had little hope that the
rules for productivity which they knew would flourish in their
son. He went on to finish his A.A. degree but did not march in
the commencement proceedings or receive his diploma. His
parents came to commencement, and he discovered that he
was sorry he had not gone through the ritual—he loved them,
and they had paid for his education.

He went to England to dig with the Royal Archeological
Society. He did so well that he was invited to go to Iran on a dig.
Then he went back to England to work with rare manuscripts
in London, following an original piece of research he designed
and proposed. He finished his B.A.

Voice III

"I got a room-and-board scholarship to Telluride House at Cornell and then didn't take it because my father got sick; there was no money, and I really didn't know what I wanted to do with education. I went to a Jungian analyst who was wise enough to tell me I needed to break away from institutions. I got a job on a trail crew at Yosemite National Park, and, the first day, walked twelve laborious miles into the high country into a strange world of men who didn't give a damn about college kids and who measured you by your ability to carry a fair share of the work. I learned more of substance about myself in those three months than perhaps any other place, and I was schooled in every four-letter, Anglo-Saxon, directive way possible. I also climbed, swam nude to a small island in a high mountain lake on a Sunday afternoon in October to celebrate my nineteenth birthday by myself, and when we broke camp ran out the twelve miles, pack on back, in an hour and 50 minutes—the only way I could give an effective and affectionate finger to my boss, an ex-Navy, ex-high school biology teacher, who had worked my butt off.

"I also met, courted spasmodically and finally, after Yosemite, married my wife, over her parents' violent objections.

"My wife and I went back to the Midwest to Iowa Wesleyan College where I majored in history and completed that major my junior year. I worked as a carpenter's helper, then contracted work, became college printer, took care of the college cars, got involved in student government, and then in a fraternity, as a political strategy—the strategy being to change the student government which was wholly Greek on a campus where almost half the students were nonfraternity. I joined with another pretheology fraternity brother in fighting to get rid of the president, newly come from the Methodist ministry. We visited the Methodist bishop in the area with representations and were happily unsuccessful. The president went on to learn to do the job well, and several years later I was honored to speak at his funeral.

"My senior year I moved to literature as a second major and had the great experience of working under the best teacher I have ever encountered. A bachelor, Yale Ph.D., Episcopalian priest who had done postgraduate work in Chaucer at Oxford. With few in his field, it was almost a private tutorial.

"My last semester I took all five of my courses with him. He taught me his love of the English language and the richness of its written expression. In June of 1967 I spoke at a testimonial dinner at IWC when he became an honorary alumnus and addressed him by his first name for the first time."

Voice I

He came from Texas via Albany, Georgia and SNCC. He was big and black, and he scared a lot of people. Not because he was threatening; he just told it like he saw it, direct and tough, and people were afraid of the dark images within themselves. He went through a number of teachers in two years. Always testing to see who was willing to understand what the world looked like through his eyes. Who would understand that you can't take white liberal ideas, or College Board scores and high school grades and tell much about the shape of a man's soul, or the urgency of his anger. It was hard to tell just how well his mind was working. What measures do you use? There was no doubt of his tenacity. He planned to be a lawyer. Some of us think he'd be a hell of a lawyer. When he left for an Outreach term to work to find teachers who would commit themselves to ghetto schools, he gave the ox yoke that he kept in the middle of his room to the president of the college. The president put it in the middle of his family room and left it there during the month of March and early April until he left Franconia.

Voice III

"Boston University School of Theology stands beside the Charles River, east of Harvard and across from M.I.T. It was, in 1954, the home of Personalism—an American humanistic brand of theology. The curriculum was rigid and, to me, arid, with the exception of Howard Thurman's "Spiritual Disciplines," Edwin Prince Booth's "Christian Biographies," and a couple of others—courses in which the spirit of the man teaching infused the content taught. I fought my way through at some expense to my soul and was probably a considerable irritation to some faculty and administrators. I learned a lot from two and a half years' field work as minister of youth in a suburban Congregational Church. The kids excited me, junior and senior high groups. They trusted me and shared a hollowness many of them felt over the current content and future prospects of their lives. I made some parents uneasy by somewhat outspoken opposition to values which they held dear.

"In my senior year, an important event occurred. I took a course in pastoral counseling at Boston State Hospital and was assigned to a paranoid schizophrenic (whatever that means) who had been in the hospital for twelve years. I read her records and naïvely suggested to myself that getting her "well" was equivalent to earning an "A." At the end of the year she was no better. I was a lot worse. A great myth had been shattered for me by the encounter with this insoluble human problem. My "patient" had built an orderly world to resolve the chaos she had encountered in her "real" life many years before and that world was closed to my concern. I was forced to acknowledge to myself that I had no better world to offer nor sufficient maturity to reach out in healing ways; more, I sensed a despair that love wouldn't be remedial in any dosage. In this failure, which others helped me work through, I learned something fundamental that no class, no book, no conversation with a teacher would ever have conveyed."

Chorus

We need some kind of supervision, firm without being authoritarian. We need a rule of law, not of personal whim. To put it bluntly, we need to say to ourselves, "Shape up or ship out."

Voice II

The board of trustees met again in Boston on March 28. At this meeting, it became evident that additional interviews had been conducted by board members at the college and in the town. It was moved that the minutes of the previous meeting —including the vote not to reappoint the president—be stricken; the motion was quickly defeated. The board began addressing the problem of an orderly transition to a different chief executive for the college.

Among the real issues discussed as reasons for dismissing the president were the failure of the college to maintain proper community relations with the town and the state; obvious dissension in the internal structure of the college; a poor image for the college because of the physical appearance of the campus; the insurance problems and the budget problems. In the eyes of the minority faction of the board, however, the president had taken on the almost impossible task of running a million-dollar business on an insufficient budget with very little help from the trustees. Objections from the minority faction that the president had answers to these charges, which the board had never heard, went unheeded. One minority member expressed his concern over the lack of time spent by the board discussing these legitimate concerns, as compared to the amount of time spent considering the accusations of the *Manchester Union-Leader* and the sometimes-anonymous local citizens. It was the view of the majority that they had consistently "dismissed" the obviously unfounded complaints of the outside world.

The board then recessed until April 1. Upon reconvening, the minority faction attempted once more—for the third time—to force reconsideration of the decision not to re-appoint the president. The attempt failed. One trustee asked the board if they would accept his resignation at this time, but it was pointed out that hasty action in a crisis situation might precipitate closing of the school. The trustee agreed to stay on the board as long as the school was kept open.

Decisions were made to ask for the president's resignation effective immediately, to appoint two board members as interim administrators empowered to enforce social rules, and to begin a search for a new president. The board recessed, to reconvene the next morning with the faculty.

Voice I

Nothing came back to the faculty from the board's meetings of March 28 and April 1 except rumors. After the April 1 meeting and before the next morning's meeting between faculty and board, the president told some of the faculty that he had walked out of the meeting that night.

It should be noted that what seemed to be at issue was not simply a marijuana raid but a whole slate of college problems: finances, student social behavior, a truculent and self-protective faculty, housekeeping, the hippie image, administrative machinery, the future of the college. The presidency was the crucial meeting place for all these issues because the board had, three years earlier, given the president total authority and total responsibility. When the combination of financial and social pressure became severe enough to embarrass the board, they snapped tight the rein on presidential responsibility; he was the only available target, the only pressure valve.

The full faculty met informally on Monday, April 1. Being unable to predict the nature of the board's previous deliberations, the faculty came up with a series of questions for the board: the nature of its concern about the presidency, what its plans were for future fund-raising, its reaction to the recent unfavorable publicity about drugs and similar, more specific requests for information. It was also suggested, since the board had requested a closed meeting, that the board be given to understand the college policy about open meetings, since several students had asked if they could attend. If, after the policy was explained, the board still requested a closed meeting, it could be closed. The faculty chairman was delegated to carry the questions and the request for an open meeting to the board.

Chorus

FRANCONIA, April 3—The fate and future of Franconia College and its president will be decided Friday morning when the board of trustees meets with members of the faculty.

The special meeting of the trustees, which opened at 10 A.M. yesterday for the prime purpose of requesting the resignation of the president of the four-year college, went into recess after a seven-hour session.

The trustees, through the chairman of the board, said the students and faculty must meet a number of conditions set by the board if the school is going to continue operations. The first condition of the board was that the president submit his resignation immediately. The trustees said two members of the faculty, two trustees and one advisory board member would be chosen to select a new president.

The second condition was that the twenty-four-hour intervisitation be curtailed. Under the present system, boys and girls are allowed "intervisitation" in college dormitory rooms.

When asked to define "intervisitation," it was explained that men and women are allowed in each other's rooms at any hour of the day or night. There are no qualifications or restrictions on the twenty-four-hour visitation period.

The trustees said they were not trying to eliminate the inter-visitation system, but only to restrict it.

Another condition laid down by the board was that the college administration take a hard line on the question of drug abuse.

The board said, "We should say we do not permit drug use, not say we don't condone it."

It was also a demand of the trustees that the college premises be cleaned up immediately. The trustees said all the dirt and dog filth must be cleaned up, not left around the rooms and walls to be walked in and tracked over the corridors.—*Manchester Union-Leader.*

Voice III

"That spring of 1965—the first of my presidency—was rough. There was no administration. That had to be built from scratch. Money was tight. Money was always tight through the next three years. Recruiting students and faculty was difficult. The decision-making process was humane but often unwieldy. Six months later, after we had graduated our first group of Associates-in-Arts degree candidates, and had grown to 250 students and twenty-nine faculty, I wrote a memo entitled, 'Some Thoughts Just Before Leaving on a Short Vacation':

> . . . somehow we have not solved enough problems yet to provide a real sense of time to teach and teach well, time for students, for discussion, for concern, for reading books and talking about important issues between students and faculty. . . ."

Voices I and III

What really kept us going with a great sense of excitement was the actual experience of teaching and working honestly with students. Most young people are so beautiful on the other side of their defenses and want so much to be beautiful without defenses. There was the young man from a broken home in Philadelphia, who grew his hair long because he liked its feel on his neck. He got accepted to Princeton and came to Franconia instead. He wrote poetry more sensitive than most and was spokesman for his graduating class.

Voice III

"From the time I took on the responsibility of the presidency, incredible ferment was the general rule at the college. Decision-making structures, student participation, academic relevancy, innovative programs, personalities, the rise of the drug culture, eternal money problems, long hair and bare feet, committee structures and powers, pets on campus, the role of community government, freedom and responsibility of students as citizens, decreasing contact with the town, physical plant needs —these were the yeasts that made the passing months fuller, trustee and town faces increasingly longer.

"There were moments when it didn't seem worthwhile. The faculty often seemed more adolescent than the students; the students often didn't seem to give a damn beyond their own personal pleasures. Abortive attempts to get townspeople and even trustees really involved finally seemed a waste of time, so I gave up putting energy into these areas. I was young, often irritable, sometimes afraid. I remember one particular dream when I felt that I was at the focal point of three forces rushing toward me: students, faculty, trustees—and at the last moment,

I jumped into the air so they could all crash headlong into each other. (Had I looked up, I would have seen the far more powerful Damoclean sword of the 'real' world—banks, insurance companies, local pressure—poised to drop as I jumped.)"

Voices I and III

There was the girl who cut her left wrist a little bit early in her freshman year. She needed someone to care about her, and that is the way she had "asked" for caring before. She was told that if she did that again she would have to leave school because she had frightened people. It was suggested to her that to be grown-up is to ask for help openly when you need it. The promise was made that she could talk any time she felt she needed to talk. She promised to and kept the promise.

Chorus

"It's a disgrace, the conditions prevailing up there, and I certainly don't condone the goings-on at that school. This behavior has got to stop. Some people in this state say there's no law above Concord, but they'll find out that there is. Once they are in this court, they're going to find out they'll get the limit."—Littleton District Court Judge Mack M. Mussman, quoted in the *Caledonia-Record*, St. Johnsbury, Vermont, March 9, 1968.

Voice II

We place this before you for your consideration. The plan is a simple one. We from the board will withdraw from this place at 11 o'clock to provide you with the full privacy you need for your discussions. We will await your decisions at 1:30, at which time the board will reconvene. We have three requests.

We do request that you release the president from this promise that he has made to you so that he will be free to resign. Second, will you tell us the consequence of your discussions and private deliberations, and then by individual vote, whether the acts, plans and programs the board has agreed upon as necessary for the continuation of the college, which we plan to put before you this morning, are such that they enlist your personal support as faculty members. And our third request, will you please appoint, not necessarily this morning but soon, two faculty members to serve with two members of the board of trustees and one member of the board of advisors to serve on a committee to search for and recommend candidates for the presidency. . . .

. . . The key to long-term funds is the continued confidence of insurance companies and banks. Presently we've lost this. We don't have it. The insurance companies have been very patient, but for a long time they've felt that this college has been a bad risk. The college, from an insurance company's viewpoint, is dirty: filth around the place, we all know there are drugs, cigarette butts everywhere, et cetera. Drugs equal violence, drugs equal weapons, et cetera. This is a bad insurance risk. They don't have to insure that type of thing. As a result there is not an insurance company that is interested in taking much of the insurance on this property. The insurance companies have come to the banks to find out if we have any insurance sources so that we could get new companies on, relieve the old companies of the risk. Of course, to the banks this raises an immediate red flag. What is going on up there? What is happening, why is it an uninsurable risk?

Chorus: Dialogue

VOICE I: And what does the board have in mind if an individual faculty member doesn't see his way clear to stating his acceptance of the program?

VOICE II: It depends on what the man says to us. . . . If some people say, "I don't like it, and to hell with it," then this is going to be a real problem. We'll deal with this as it comes up. We've got to conform with it, or we've got to close.

Voice I

The meeting of April 2 was well-attended by faculty, and students were also present. The board had asked for a closed meeting; it turned out later that the message hadn't gotten to them. After the chairman presented the board's three requests, he turned the floor over to the board's financial expert, who spelled out in detail the severity of the college's financial and insurance problems, thereby offering proof that the threat of immediate closure was indeed real. Then the chairman told the faculty that immediate steps must be taken to deal effectively with the problems of twenty-four-hour intervisitation, drugs, noise in student housing, "dogs, dirt, and defacement," fire hazards, local public relations, and "housing."

The board's first request was the first concrete word we had gotten of the forced resignation. The faculty, after its initial shock subsided, elected a five-man committee which, with three students, would meet with the board to attempt to work out solutions that would in some measure preserve the autonomy of the college and still satisfy the board. This "negotiating" committee met with and extracted from the board agreement to recess from 5:00 P.M. on Tuesday until 10:00 A.M. on Friday, April 5, at which time the negotiating committee would present to the board models for college reorganization which would meet the board's "grave concerns" and still maintain some level of internal confidence within the college.

The board went home; the community mobilized. The problem was no longer the college we wanted versus the college they wanted; it was a problem of keeping any kind of college at all. Students swept through all campus property, cleaning, painting and repairing. People actually took their pets home. The negotiating committee appointed some seventeen sub-committees to draw up proposals for revised reorganization to meet every aspect of the board's "grave concerns", and for implementation of those revisions on a student-faculty level. Something like 160 people worked, virtually nonstop, from Tuesday night until Friday morning, hammering on a final draft of thirty-odd pages, printing it in the college print shop and getting it to the 10:00 A.M. meeting. No classes were missed; academic business went on as usual. Martin Luther King, Jr. was murdered that Thursday evening, and the cities began to burn. The college scheduled a memorial service for the next Monday.

Northern New Hampshire is a curious part of a curious country at a curious time. On Tuesday night after the board had presented its ultimatums to the community, the townspeople formed a vigilante committee to protect their homes. The National Guard's closest unit was alerted, and the state police were asked to come into the area in case of trouble. To protect the town from the college students. The students did not, of course, riot and burn. They never have, and I doubt they ever will. They were too busy—mopping, painting, cutting each others' hair—trying to protect their college from the town. And from the trustees, banks, insurance companies, media and the police —all of whom had already indicated a certain hostile intent.

The negotiating committee's final plan was submitted to the community and accepted by a vote of 163 to 7. It recommended retention of the president in a faculty position under faculty control and withdrawal of the board's request for signed statements of faculty support for the board's programs. It also proposed a "social standards committee" to help implement the board's wishes with regard to the "social problems." Nobody was happy about the plan; nobody wanted to give up on any last possibility of keeping the college open.

On Friday morning, the *Manchester Union-Leader*'s "Bare Debauchery" story hit the town. It didn't help anybody's frame of mind. The negotiating committee presented its case and the document to the board and then withdrew to await word from the trustees. When the trustees called them back about five hours later, the committee was handed a statement drawn up by the board, expressing approval of the good work of the committee and the student body and delineating the conditions which the board would accept for continued operation of the school.

The retention of the president in any office or in any connection in the employ of the school was flatly rejected. The trustees withdrew the request for signed statements of support. They accepted the "spirit" of the committee's plan but no specific proposals with regard to social governance. A compromise statement was worked out regarding faculty rights "to its role in the recruitment and selection of faculty and to the election of its own officers." During the afternoon session, the phone kept ringing (the trustees were meeting at a member's house because they were afraid security might be violated again if they met at the school—they blamed the faculty, rightly so, one supposes, for opening up the April 2 meeting); the negotiating committee was informed that a board member was sitting on three phone calls from three banks, threatening foreclosure if immediate action wasn't taken on the question of the presidency. The committee crumbled. The statement of the board of trustees, accepting the modified plan "in spirit but not in detail" was taken back up the hill and presented to the community; the negotiating committee stood mute, recommending neither acceptance nor rejection. Neither was called for. The board of trustees went back to the problem of trying to hold off the insurance companies and mortgage holders.

Voice II

I pointed out that if the college closed, the outside forces would have achieved a victory. As it was, the antipresident forces had won. The members of the negotiating committee realized that the board could not be reasoned with and that to save the battle for another day, they had to capitulate to every demand. It seemed unfair that a group used to confronting one another over problems never had an opportunity to confront the spectres of the banks, insurance companies and the surrounding community. In fact, the board never confronted these powers. Even though the board felt that sacrificing the president would restore the confidence of the insurance companies, they were mistaken. The insurance had been cancelled on Thursday, April 4, and was not reinstated, the board felt, as a result of the open meeting. All efforts by influential board members failed to reverse the insurance companies' decision. The present insurance was purchased from companies not previously handling Franconia College.

The reading of the statement by the board to the college community was anticlimactic. I returned home and cried hard for half an hour.

Voice I

Things went rather sour after that. The students began dropping by the registrar's office, requesting transcripts for transfer purposes. Two members of the administrative staff resigned. The peculiarly independent nature of Franconia's last two years —the Oxford-style upper division—is such that transfer out without loss of credit is difficult if a student is at the beginning of his senior year. Faculty members began calling on friends at other experimental colleges to accept promising students. The faculty began circulating resumes. Not all the faculty, of course, or all the students, wanted out. To some, the enforced acceptance of an external hand was welcome. Franconia College's processes have never been neat enough for some of its members.

Voice III

"Obviously, the variety of my educational background has influenced the assumptions I worked from at Franconia, assumptions which were strengthened or modified by these five intense years. It seems increasingly to me that *people* are the critical factor in education. The human environment around the student really conditions what is educative, rather than curricular structures or specific course content.

"The attempt to divide intellectual (academic) and emotional (social) behavior of students is one of higher education's most serious problems. Ruling out emotional behavior as a proper concern of the teacher in his classroom and of the academic dean in his curricular planning invites the motivational problems so often discussed *vis-à-vis* intellectual endeavor. It continues a dualism of mind and body which seems inappropriate to the young and produces an overreaction on their part—an overreaction described as antiintellectual in character, but which is more the failure of an untrained intellect. A skilled mind is a necessity for ordering and dealing creatively with the world, just as mature emotions are needed to experience the world.

"I contend that answer-oriented, success-directed education does not lead to a skilled intellect, since it sharply cuts off the mind from the emotions which drive it.

"A second critical problem is to reintroduce failure as a positive force in collegiate curriculums. It is not easy to acknowledge failures in the United States, much less explore and learn from them. Perfection *is* an unattainable goal in life, and the illusion created by the insistent demand for it is an enemy of growth. Growth is, after all, the ostensible point of all education. Disagreements are over what kind or what balance of growth is most valuable, and, more basic, in what ways to achieve growth.

"Freud opened up the question of the source of both creativity and destructiveness. He identified this source with sexuality. So the goal of education becomes a problem of sexual maturity in the fullest sense. Fucking (read as in *Lady Chatterly;* to probe with full being, not just the mind) is for deepening love or making babies, otherwise it becomes a form of mutual masturbation or rape. In very much the same way, a truly creative mind fucks the richness of ideas and experience, both personal and historical, as a way of knowing what exists and of creating unique variations—creating, in fact, newness. This is what scholarship is about. This is what students should be about. This is what colleges should be about. This is how life is sustained. Then and only then will a student be able to choose in the classroom with the same deep enthusiasm with which he chooses in the bedroom. Then and only then will students (all of us) discover that ethics is the art of distinguishing between healthy fucking and masturbation or rape, which destroy. To choose to act in ways which give health is a choice not of abstract metaphysics, traditional morality codes, Emily Post, or the law of the land, but a choice to be fully a man or woman. The source of ethics must always be what is discovered as best between two humans. Law must always be a reflection of that discovery.

"This is perhaps why the general double standard of "adult" America, exposed in its real dimensions by the Kinsey report of 1954, is so repugnant to the young. The 'real' world *is* whitewashed without, corrupt within, and the corruption is corrupt because it is white-washed self-deceit, rather than coming from inherently evil acts or intentions behind the façade. The 'real' world does have twenty-four-hour intervisitation, is semi- or completely addicted to its own post-Volstead Act legalized narcotic; it does lie, cheat, steal, destroy, evade or ignore the law when it serves the adult's individual purpose. Many young people are refusing to use these 'facts' as excuses for their own behavior. They are saying, 'We will neither do what you do, nor do what you say, since what you do and what you say don't square, and don't, in your suburban life, produce joy and love or creative thoughts and products.'

"Students are increasingly Socratic in their perception of life. You know only what you do (baby), and you judge people by what they *do*, not what they say.

"For vast numbers of the young, the old stories—whether Judaic, Catholic, Protestant, Marxist, capitalist or academic— are functionally dead as significant guides to living a meaningful life, and these young men and women are desperately engaged in trying to learn how to tell who they are and what they can do by being honest about themselves and their weaknesses— through living and learning from the unfolding story of their own lives. They do not want or feel they need someone to be responsible for them. They want to be responsible for themselves. Supported in this, believed in, worked with and provided with real jobs to do, their incredible energies could be constructively loosed to solve the real problems of fear (and its overt manifestation, hate).

"Student phrases today are 'Where are you at?' and 'What's your bag?' They mean, who are you (what is your story) and what can you do? Because the young basically distrust their parents' world, telling their own stories is difficult without therapy. And so education must concern itself with therapy— value, personal, work and play therapy—and through this therapy reaffirm that man has produced nothing greater than the individual man or woman who is free, responsible and creative. Reaffirm, too, that the goal of a society is to enhance the trip from the cradle to the grave, the only trip which is truly involved in consciousness expansion, a trip most truly taken *with* others, not for them or because of them. This trip can best be taken without using people, things, ideas, beliefs and drugs as crutches or security blankets.

"And all of this can happen when the attitudes of adults establish an environment which accepts the young as people, rejecting destructive behavior without rejecting the person. Unless we accept that the 'real' world as we find it is right, then we must find ways of fighting the organized lovelessness inherent in most institutions. We must affirm that the life of one baby —black, brown, yellow, red, white—is worth more than the grandest, noblest nonhuman creation of man. A child is not a potential component for an organizational mechanism: a child is a life to be lived.

"The conservation of our young people is the most important task facing this country. The future is the only resource we have, and the future belongs to the children. When you conserve a forest, you do so by stopping people from cutting down the trees, not by requiring that the trees grow in a prescribed way. So it should be with education.

"The dangers inherent in my viewpoint are obvious. It is impossible utopianism. People are already under more pressure than they can bear: put enough pressure on a man and his ability to tolerate ambiguity diminishes rapidly and is replaced by an all-consuming desire for almost any order at any cost. Such a man, when he can no longer control change or stop change in his immediate environment, will use and manipulate institutions (the government, law, police, military, banks, insurance companies) to satisfy his need for order above all else. This has always been the danger of American pragmatism. In times of crisis, order becomes the greatest good, the ultimate good, which *is* to make means an end.

I am convinced that it is precisely at this focal point that the decline and fall or renewal of this country rests. It is one thing when the young cut themselves off from their elders (which they are doing); it is a totally different situation when, through fear, the elders in a society cut themselves off from the young. If we don't do something about the generation gap, it will become (rapidly *is* becoming) an abyss into which this nation will fall.

"The responsibility for initiating a change in this coldest of all wars rests with those of us who are older. We must resign from the future we have dreamed about and failed to reach, and move toward a new understanding with (not of) our kids. Because we are the ones who have the skills to help the young implement their dreams. There is no life without dreams, no living without implementation. The process of planning, which we have come to understand as vital in a time of exploding population and rapid technological change, can be used for any end, and the definition of those ends rightly belongs to those who are going to live with the results the longest."

Yevtushenko, in his poem, "Lies," best sums it up:

> Telling lies to the young is wrong.
> Proving to them that lies are true is wrong.
> Telling that God's in his heaven
> and all's well with the world is wrong.
> The young know what you mean. The young are people.
> Tell them the difficulties can't be counted,
> and let them see not only what will be
> but see with clarity these present times.
> Say obstacles exist they must encounter,
> sorrow happens, hardship happens.
> The hell with it. Who never knew
> the price of happiness will not be happy.
> Forgive no error you recognize,
> it will repeat itself, increase,

and afterwards our pupils
will not forgive in us what we forgave.*

Voices I and III

The crisis at Franconia College was one of confidence at three
levels. There was the question of the internal confidence of the
school—the faith between the students, the teachers and the
administrators that we were all working for the same things.
There was the question of local confidence—within the village,
the surrounding towns, within the state of New Hampshire; this
was the confidence upon which the real (in the sense of real
estate) strength of the school was built. And there was the confidence of the larger academic world—the confidence of the
nation, as it were.

Confidence failed on the second level, and this is where the
college's base lay. Its financing, its insurance, its protection from
fear-engendered attack. The board of trustees decided—were
forced—to rebuild this confidence at any cost. They sacrificed
internal confidence quickly; the actions taken appeased the
vindictive, reassured the hysterical—and gutted the faculty and
student body. The solutions were short-term, aimed at surviving another month, another week. The hysterical will be hysterical again, if not over drugs, sex, beards, dirt, dogs, or chaos,
then over books or words.

But accusations are pointless, since the choice was forced and
the alternatives nonexistent. The left wing of the faculty saw
clearly that death—closing the school—was infinitely preferable to surrender of principle. Saw it almost as clearly as the right
wing saw that order must be installed or death was inevitable.
The middle-ground has probably won, for now, the responsibil-

* *Yevtushenko: Selected Poems* (New York: E. P. Dutton, 1962). Copyright
© 1962 by Robin Milner-Gulland and Peter Levi. Reprinted by permission of
E. P. Dutton & Co., Inc.

ity of either fighting the battle to get the college back, or watching the slow erosion of the rest of the school's autonomy.

The question of the third level of confidence remains, one of many open-ended questions to arise from Franconia College's experiences of March and April, 1968. American higher education respects institutions that are tough, independent, autonomous; how severely the profession will judge Franconia's desperate struggle for life remains to be seen.

Epilogue

Franconia College did not die, of course. The dispute with the board worsened during the subsequent summer, and nineteen faculty members tendered their resignations—although two or three still teach there, three years later. An acting president was appointed, lasted two eventful years and then was replaced by a twenty-three-year-old whiz who seems destined to get the school on sound financial footing.

During the acting president's reign, the *Manchester Union-Leader* filed suit against the college, freezing its assets. In a desperate financial bind, the administration settled out of court —by virtue of publishing a statement which admitted that all of the *Union-Leader*'s allegations concerning the college were true. Thus does one purchase one's "freedom"—in this case freedom to survive—in our free society.

And thus the students got one more lesson in "relevancy" and "interaction with the real world" and those other shibboleths of the educational revolution. They discovered one more vital area where it's okay to talk about honesty, but of course things don't *work* that way. The bill comes due, and you pay it. Somehow, with something—honor, trust, freedom, principals. You'll be more careful next time, of course. You'll have to be. Isn't that the way we educated you?

IV State University of New York College at Old Westbury

What we failed to achieve—but kept hoping we were just about to achieve—was the minimum mutual understanding necessary to make the partnership of faculty, students and administration work. What we discovered was the depth of our disagreements . . . and our negative insights were not enough.

HARRIS WOFFORD

DREAMS AND REALITIES
How Big the Wave?

HARRIS WOFFORD

This section does not contain a "Dreams" portion, as Harris Wofford's essay about Old Westbury includes numerous passages from the original planning data for the college. Mr. Wofford now serves as president of Bryn Mawr College.

College-making is something like surf-riding. The critical factors are one's own skill, timing, and judgment and the size, shape, and speed of the wave. Looking back on the story of the new College at Old Westbury, 1966–70, we can see how bad was our footwork, and how big the wave. We sorely underestimated the wave of student discontent and the difficulties of liberal education in this turbulent sea. Our hope was that the State University's experimental college could ride the wave then rolling out of Berkeley. If discontent didn't exist, we said, a good college would need to stir it up. We tried to ride the wave and fell, and tried and fell, and tried and fell.

> In creating this new college the State University sees the restlessness, curiosity and questioning of youth not as a spectre but an opportunity. The turbulent, critical mood of today's students is a great occasion for education.

That is what we said in our first catalog in 1967. I would say it again, but as the poet says, "Set down this, set down this: . . . a cold coming we had of it." We opened the State University's new experimental college in the fall of 1968 with poetry reading; my contribution was Marvell's *To His Coy Mistress*. We would roll all our strength and all our sweetness into one ball and make the sun run.

After a too turbulent year, culminating in a student sit-in with the slogan "Paranoia is True Perception," I ended the year reading Eliot's *Journey of the Magi*. That winter of discontent, following the killings of Robert Kennedy and Martin Luther King, Jr. and the spread of the war in Vietnam, was the worst time for a trip like ours. Was it a birth or a death?

There was a death certainly. We who had started the college so boldly concluded three years later that the first pilot program should be "phased out" and a new administration given a chance to start afresh. But that is not necessarily a measure of failure. Phoenix-like, Old Westbury may be destined for many rebirths. We had warned the university that it should expect an experimental college to fail regularly in some of its experiments; then to give a candid account of what had been learned. Indeed, we often told ourselves that we would rather fail big than succeed small; from such a failure much might be learned. And much needs to be learned about how to reach, attract and teach the new student generation.

What was learned in the rise and fall of Old Westbury's first program?

From the distance of a year and miles that can't be measured between Old Westbury and Bryn Mawr, it is still painful to remember the original hopes and to ask what went wrong, or to ask what went right and to recall how close we seemed to making the experiment work.

The simplest conclusion is a negative paradox: it was all leaven and no lump. One of the troubles with experimental colleges is that they attract too many experimental people.

And if the experiment includes "full partnership" with students in a time of student rebellion, when consent everywhere is withering, the trouble is compounded. For us it meant that issues of student power regularly overshadowed and overwhelmed study, teaching or curriculum planning. Participatory democracy—as H. G. Wells said of socialism—takes too many evenings.

But that is too simple. The old lump—the existing educational establishment—wasn't working well either. What drew to Old Westbury a man devoted to curriculum innovation like Byron Youtz, physicist and acting-president of Reed College, was the belief that with student participation we could escape the political confrontations increasingly consuming other campuses and turn our "full creative powers to meaningful exchange with students, to research and to artistry."

That was the promise in the university's 1966 master plan. Conceived as a constructive response to Berkeley, a way for New York to get ahead of any such explosion, the new college for five thousand students would "pay heed to the individual student and his concern with the modern world"; "end the lock-step march in which one semester follows on another until four of youth's most energetic years have been consumed," and "admit students to full partnership in the academic world."

In our high hopes, we saw the new student generation as a giant Socrates, beard and all, come to sting conventional educaton into the necessary reforms. In the first statement of Old Westbury's program we said:

> Their complaints against the multiversity, their concern
> for relevance, their search for individual identity and their
> questioning of everything can lead to better teaching,
> more relevant courses, more disciplined and serious study,
> deeper understanding and greater involvement with pub-
> lic problems.

So with students invited as "full partners," we did our best to plan a college that would be a collective Socrates for the whole of the State University, if not all of American higher education.

Pride goes before a fall. Our best was not enough. We and the new college were the first ones stung by our student gadflies, and it hurt.

Even that was predictable, for Socratic dialectic is supposed to puncture pretenses. What we failed to achieve—but kept hoping we were just about to achieve—was the minimum mutual understanding necessary to make the partnership of faculty, students and administration work. What we discovered was the depth of our disagreements. We shared criticisms of conventional academia but differed much more than we expected on the reforms necessary; and our negative insights were not enough.

In announcing my appointment, the then Chancellor of the University, Samuel Gould, said that he had asked us "to review all the conventional ingredients such as admissions policies, grades, course systems and academic divisions and break whatever barriers may stand in the way."

The biggest barriers, it turned out, were not in the system but in ourselves. Let me describe some of the steps that led to this conclusion with this *caveat:* the Old Westbury story is a *Rashomon* with as many different accounts as there were participants.

Phase One

Over twenty months of planning began for me in the summer of 1966 when I first walked the 600 acres of woods and steeple chase fields of the late F. Ambrose Clark on which a hundred million dollar campus was to be constructed. The words of the university master plan ran in my head:

> Since the campus is to be built literally from the ground up,
> the president and the faculty members the president re-
> cruits will have an almost unrestricted opportunity for in-
> novation and creativity.

It was an opportunity one is unlikely to get twice in a lifetime.
But the lonely intoxication could not last, for the opportunity
had to be shared with colleagues—"the president and the
faculty members the president recruits," said the master plan.
I thought we also needed to recruit some students right away.
If the promised partnership of faculty, students and administration were to be a reality, students should be involved in the
planning and not arrive to find a near-finished product. Old
Westbury should not be a planned college, but a college that
plans; its policies should not percolate down, but be framed
with the participation of all its constituencies. We should, therefore, start with a live nucleus of the real thing, a planning staff
including all three constituencies.

This may have been the first of our miscalculations for we
were not ready to deal with the seven student planners we
recruited. They came from Antioch, Berkeley, Goddard, San
Francisco State, and Stonybrook and ranged from a 17-year-old
freshman drop-out to graduate students and an ex-Peace Corps
volunteer in their mid-twenties. Professor Lawrence Resnick,
an analytical philosopher whose critical guard was usually high,
confessed later that in selecting some of the first students he
preferred the discontented and rejected the square: the former
interesting, the latter boring him.

In selecting the first faculty we no doubt applied a similar
bias. Teaching stars on their campuses, champions of student
protest and academic reform, they were interesting critics, not
necessarily good builders. Together we lacked the oil of apathy
that keeps most institutions running.

From our first planning seminars, divisions were evident, and
much of the diversity was deliberate, *mea culpa*. I had re-

cruited several colleagues from the Peace Corps and several who shared the experience of great books seminars at the University of Chicago or St. John's College; then since none of us came out of the regular circle of college faculties or academic disciplines, two tenured full professors and several younger academics were added, all with their own, quite different educational viewpoints. Very quickly some of our new colleagues made it clear that their interest in educational reform notwithstanding, they viewed those with Ph.D.s as the only true faculty and intended to protect the rights of their guild against abridgement by administrators.

We should not have expected that a thousand years of academic politics would miraculously subside, but I had hoped that the magic of our unusual assignment would forestall it. From the relative success of a similar process in the first years of the Peace Corps, which some of us saw as a potential University in Dispersion, I had undue confidence that a group of intelligent men and women with strongly differing visions could, through a wide open dialogue, create an institution which had that process of dialogue at its core. My optimistic American pluralism was showing.

Robert Hutchins, Stringfellow Barr, and Scott Buchanan, three of the main teachers in my past, warned me against this "good men" fallacy. Good ideas are what count, they urged; make sure that your educational program is very clear and that everyone you ask to join you understands and agrees. Since they knew that Chicago after World War II had been a golden time for me, and that I considered the full great books curriculum the hardest and probably best in the United States, I suspected that they wanted me to take up their banner and simply carry on where they left off. But they had been designing and testing that curriculum for years before they raised their banner, and even so, Hutchins' college had been blown away. Buchanan and

Barr, when they left St. John's, said that all they had started was a search for the true liberal college.

Our assignment, it seemed to me, was to continue the search, and try to do better than any of these earlier programs. Having an idea of combining St. John's and Antioch, Chicago and the Peace Corps, but with no clear-cut program to impose, I felt the need to assemble a group of varied experience and approaches. I was counting also upon the larger dialectic of events to teach and unite us, a form of learning-by-doing, learning-while-college-making. But the warnings turned out to be well taken: the disillusion and depression of the spirit of the late sixties tended instead to pull us apart, and the program I was proposing was not compelling enough to hold our disparate group together.

Nevertheless, with persistence and a high level of passion, the twenty of us met for most of 1967 as an almost daily roundtable on liberal education. We explored what had been our own best educational experiences. We considered the experiences of a number of previous experimental colleges. We consulted scores of educators, and we read and discussed dozens of books. From Alfred North Whitehead's *The Aims of Education,* one of our main texts, we accepted the prescription that the first year of a college should take students by surprise, break the grip of conventional wisdom and cause them to stand up and start questioning the world; we sought to apply his proposed stages of learning—romance, specialization and generalization—to our first curriculum; and we took as an overall theme (and the cover statement for our first catalog) this dictum:

> The tragedy of the world is that those who are imaginative have but slight experience, and those who are experienced have feeble imaginations. Fools act on imagination without knowledge, pedants act on knowledge without imagination. The task of a university is to weld together imagination and experience.

To the surprise of those of us whose most recent experience was overseas in the Peace Corps, the imagination of the student planners focused almostly entirely on domestic problems of race and poverty. Their turning away from distant adventures in the City of Man and turning inward to the American inner city was a sign of the times, probably an early by-product of the then expanding Vietnam war.

Old Westbury would be a "School of the World," I had said in an early announcement, and we did agree upon some international dimensions. We planned a program for some twenty students in Israel, involving work in kibbutzim; we said we would seek large numbers of foreign students and faculty; and we provided that students could spend a year or more in overseas programs. But our major field activities were to be in urban assignments at home. The main first program emerged as a work-study, education-in-action curriculum, with terms of field work on urban problems and with small social science and humanities seminars continuing during off-campus as well as on-campus terms. "Old Westbury proposes to be a 'school of the world' in the broad sense of the word world: the world students will go out into, defined by its problems," we agreed to say in the catalog. "Take any of our major domestic concerns—urbanization, education, integration, automation, poverty—and they turn out to be world-wide problems."

From the beginning the idea of great books seminars was a source of central controversy. "Can't you just call them 'very good books'?" asked one of the student planners. Those of us pressing the books capitulated on the rhetorical point: the Bible was a very good book, Shakespeare quite a good writer. But we were insistent that reading the major books of civilization, and discussing them in seminars, was an essential part of what we meant by a liberal education. For those of us who had experienced the power of a community of faculty and students reading and discussing such works, the idea of some kind of required common seminar was crucial. This raised the issue of common requirements of any kind. For most of the student planners and some faculty, anything "common" was an imposition.

After long argument, we reached what seemed a reasonable and novel compromise: there would be required "common humanities seminars," constituting one-third of the curriculum; they would consist of some fifteen students led by two faculty members of different academic specialties; about half the reading list would be prescribed in advance by a joint faculty-student committee, but the other half would be free for each seminar to determine as it went along.

The underlying issue, however, was unresolved. For some faculty members such seminars ran against the grain of the academic specialism in which they believed. I will never forget the disaster of the planning staff's seminar on *Antigone*. Aside from a stoned or otherwise high student who insisted on first reading aloud an irrelevant ribald piece, we did not get far before our Doctor of Philosophy in Literature exploded: he could not let us talk about *Antigone* as amateurs when he *knew* the background, the subtlety and the significance of the play; he would tell us about it. He could not accept the idea that the "teacher" for the evening was Sophocles, not any professor present.

For students it was not our amateurism but our "authoritarianism" that they suspected. In a perceptive account, student planner Ralph Keyes of Antioch told of a question I asked the planning staff: "Isn't it true, or likely to be true, that there are *some* things which *every* person needs to learn in order to be free, things as essential to our minds and souls as water and salt, bread and wine are to our bodies?" "No!" Keyes reported, was "the cry from student planners across the table."

Hip students today (and Old Westbury's students *are* hip)
almost instinctively grimace when promised a "common
course." Individuality is the program, and dated talk of
"community" conflicts with their alienated near-nihilism.
Raised permissively and educated progressively, they
argue passionately for a do-your-own-thing style of education. These students have been raised on New Math, New
Physics, history by sources and politics by experience. Pre-
college training today is so rigorous, television so broaden-
ing and drugs so mind-expanding that contemporary
college students are scornful of mind-body separation.
They've turned on, sampled sex, trained their sensitivity,
grooved with light shows and are not about to be told that
growth occurs best by slithering an idea around a seminar
table.

That stated the issue. "Whether this current is a good one is
not the point," concluded Keyes. "It is there, runs deep and
won't succumb easily to pleading." It *was* the point for some of
us, but Ralph was right that the current runs deep.

Professor Resnick rebutted in satire, with his memo,
"Progressive Education at Winterhole":

Here, amid the murmuring pines, ten thousand babies
crawl around educating themselves at their own pace.
Nurtured by a deep commitment to the philosophical ideal
of personal freedom, they are not subject to inhibitions of
rules or mores from an oppressive society. Since there is no
such thing as teaching, Winterhole has no teachers at all.
Inner motivation is the only source of learning. Director
A.S. Schlemiel fondly recalls the story of Freddy, who at
thirteen had not yet decided to learn to control his
sphincter muscles. In fact, at this writing, Freddy is
twenty-one and has not yet made the inner commitment.
Proud, but soiled, Freddy crawls through life (he has not
yet decided to learn to walk either), a truly free man.

Out of the smoke came the agreed-upon program that combined an unusually large requirement of common seminars *and*

an unusually large freedom for independent study and off-campus field work, a promising alloy I thought. "It's oil and water," warned Ralph Keyes. Today's students, he predicted, "will revolt, and when they do, the way Old Westbury responds will determine what kind of institution it becomes. Call it softness or call it decency: Old Westbury will end up allowing students to do their thing."

The student revolt had in fact begun the day the first student planners arrived and asked that all decision making be on the basis of one planner, one vote. From the beginning they were fully participating members of the planning staff and indeed soon comprised about half of those sitting at our almost daily planning roundtable, then our only decision-making process. When committees were formed, the student planners were full members of every committee. Throughout the planning period we proceeded largely by consensus without votes, although we often noted that the day would come when a faculty would begin to exercise major academic responsibilities, and I repeatedly affirmed the president's considerable powers and duties under the rules of the State University.

Not satisfied, the students pressed for a formal democratic structure recognizing much more far-reaching student power over curriculum, appointments and budget. Not convinced that they were prepared for such power or that majoritarian principles were appropriate for academic governance, a number of us resisted. I soon found myself saying "No" much of the time.

No, partnership meant participation but did not mean blurring the separate roles of faculty, students, and administration. No, the president would not be merely a chairman, servant, or technician for the prevailing majority. No, decisions would not be made through a process in which students outnumber faculty and administration. No, the first student planners would not automatically become members of the faculty, as one soon demanded.

"Betrayal!" and "Hypocrisy!" were the student counter-charges, moderated by the fact that they knew they had in-fluenced the first program in major respects and by the close friendships that developed. "You can't fight so well against a president when you call him by his first name," one student told a reporter. Or, as another student put it, leaving after a friendly night: "I knew I shouldn't have come to dinner. It's going to ruin our confrontation tomorrow."

Youth's urge to rebel is indeed a deep current, as most parents know. Raised permissively, many of today's students find the university their first good target, a natural free firing zone. One of the student planners confessed that the protest syndrome is so strong among his peers that when an administration provides little cause to revolt, in frustration they turn elsewhere. "At Antioch last year we almost hung the barber," he said. Old Westbury was supposed to demonstrate how teachers and administrators should deal with this.

Not believing our first student planners were representative, we decided to take another probe of students, and add some new "partners" who might respond more affirmatively. In the summer of 1967 we arranged a workshop for students chosen from the campuses of the State University on special scholarships provided by Chancellor Gould and announced through the regular campus student body organizations. When those thirteen students arrived from colleges like Geneseo, New Paltz and Potsdam, we hoped the voices of moderation and practicality would at last be heard. Either Old Westbury immediately went to their heads or they were as alienated from academia, scholarship and all forms of American authority as the first group.

"Just come to Potsdam," one kept saying as proof of his sweeping indictments. Their educational platform was much the same: action against injustice, exploration of psyches and the anarchy of no requirements, no evaluation and everyone doing his thing (except the president). When Chancellor Gould came to hear their criticisms and proposals, they rested their case on the playing of Bob Dylan's song, "There's something going on here but you don't know what it is, do you Mr. Jones?" And their response to the promise of "full partnership" was even wilder: although they were only going to be with us for part of one summer they thought they should have equal votes in all decision making. "You've got the bull by the horns," Chancellor Gould said as he left. "Good luck!"

With these danger signals, why did we push on and open the college in 1968? It was not just the courage of our overconfidence. We hardly knew how to stop. Published accounts of "The College That Students Helped Plan" flooded us with applicants. Attractive, idealistic, insistent that Old Westbury was the only place for them, hundreds came for interviews and applicant seminars. We told ourselves that with the student planners we had wrestled with the most intense spirit of the times, and we were now ready for whatever came. Nor had the planning phase been without fun.

After the heat of argument, most of the student planners, including the most critical, wanted to stay with us or return; one joined the full-time staff, one (the drop-out) applied and was later admitted as a student. Ralph Keyes concluded that the college would succeed. Asked why, he said:

> I am tempted to fumble about like Sancho Panza when asked what he saw in Don Quixote, then sing out, "I like him!" And Old Westbury *is* an immensely likeable place. It just has a good feel about it. For what Old Westbury does offer, more than any other college I know, is a rare collection of decent, flexible, compassionate human beings.

A prospective faculty member was persuaded the college was something very special when he was interviewed by one of the thirteen summer student planners, then back studying on his campus; the student stated that after getting his Ph.D. he expected to join the Old Westbury faculty himself. No matter how honestly and pessimistically we conveyed our difficulties, prospective faculty almost invariably found the candor or liveliness appealing.

When we planned an all-day series of seminars for a hundred prospective student applicants from Long Island, our student planners at lunch surprised us all with a "happening" of lights, slides, balloons, ballet-dancing and a taped speech of mine overlaid with ridiculous music. A local newspaper editor's mind did seem "blown," but in describing it in her paper she fortunately mistook black-bearded Allen Ginsberg, whose giant poster dominated the ballroom, for Uncle Sam. Often luck seemed to be with us.

During this period, Professor Resnick was even uncharacteristically encouraging. "Part of the charm, fascination, frustration and education of the place is that it can't be captured," he wrote. "It's off-balance and open; nothing is sacred, not even the passionately held educational views of its president." But he added:

> If Old Westbury succeeds it will not be because we allow each student to do his thing. It will be because we interest the students in the processes of discovery, confusion and rediscovery which, however crudely, we have tried to use in the planning of the college.

We hoped to succeed partly because we thought we had a scheme for organic growth that would institutionalize this process of discovery, confusion and rediscovery and do it less crudely. We agreed that Old Westbury would be a "college of colleges." We would start our first program with only eighty-five students, growing to several hundred, with an interdisciplinary faculty of around thirty developing one set of curricular ideas. This would be our first constituent college. Then we would start a second, contrasting program and a third, fourth, fifth. Together, in competition and coordination, these constituent colleges would constitute a continuing dialogue on the best ways and means of teaching and learning the liberal arts. The classical model for a college of colleges, of course, is Oxford or Cambridge. The nearest American analogue was the University of California's new campus at Santa Cruz with its several colleges organized around different academic themes.

We had another reason for an early start before the 1,000-student campus was completed and ready to be filled. "Start small," John Gardner, then Secretary of Health, Education and Welfare had advised me. He considered the biggest problem in higher education the departmentalization that cuts up the body of knowledge and keeps us from seeing the world steady and whole. The most important task is to find a better form of organization than departments. If departments ever get going at Old Westbury, he predicted, you will never be able to eliminate them. Start so small that departments don't make any sense, he urged, and in doing this you may discover the right alternative; you may rediscover the liberal college.

"Beware of the small, smothering, ingrown, incestuous, utopian community," warned Webster College's Sister Jacqueline Grennan (now Mrs. Paul Wexler, president of Hunter College). Then in the process of secularizing herself and her college, she spent several months at Old Westbury as a regular consultant. "Start big," she said, "with enough different programs, with enough variety of students and faculty and living and working relationships so that you will reflect and confront the real world, instead of falling into the mock heroics of utopia." She urged us to enroll a high proportion of local community college graduates in order to counteract the tendency to attract primarily utopian types.

In planning the architecture we did take Jacqueline's advice: the architects, in close collaboration with our planning staff, designed five clusters for 1,000 students each, seeking the maximum feasible diversity in living and learning arrangements. We said it had to accomodate our proposed "college of colleges," without academic departments or a more conventional organization in case our program was replaced. It may win prizes for flexibility.

But we did not take the warning against utopianism seriously enough, soon enough. We didn't appreciate the enormous appeal of just the general banner of an experimental college and the special appeal of a college with students as full partners. Even as the student applications mounted into the thousands, we did not recognize the degree to which we were drawing the utopians or recognize their drawbacks for a new college: their expectations are very high but they also get very disappointed.

This skewing of our population threw a shadow on our proposed curriculum that we didn't see in time. The work-study program with a freshman semester in the inner-city had been designed for what we expected to be still relatively conventional, though above-average, mostly suburban students of New York State. We thought it would "break the grip" of suburbia and lead these students into a more examined life. Too late, we realized that most of the students we were attracting—and perhaps a majority of students applying today to any above-average college—were already too turned-on, too much at loose ends for their good or ours. En route to Old Westbury, somewhere in the assassinations, riots, wars, trips to the moon, television and drugs through which they had lived, established society's grip on them seemed already to have been broken and with it their grip on the world.

Unhappily, we did not really understand this until educated by the events of the first year of full operation. If we had sensed the chaos in the students' minds, I hope we would have found a way to offer more of the order, structure and intellectual leadership they needed. Whether they would have taken that is another question. What most of them thought they needed was power, a chance to experiment with new life-styles and a place of sympathy and encouragement for their personal growth. For some of us this was a far cry from the liberal education we saw as their most critical need and the central concern of a college.

Meanwhile, someone up there may have been telling us something. A few days after Martin King's assassination in the spring of 1968, a fire started accidentally on the roof of our administration building where all this planning had taken place. We watched it burn to the ground and take with it almost all our records, planning documents and personal papers of a lifetime.

Phase Two

The first formal academic year, 1968–1969, came fast after the fire.

In early summer, ten new faculty members arrived along with some dozen students on student-aid jobs around campus. Hearing about a three-week faculty preparatory session, the students demanded, unsuccessfully, that all decision making cease until the full student body arrived; then they wrote their fellow-students to hurry along, with bedrolls and tents if necessary, to keep the faculty and administration from making all the decisions. Faced with its first challenge from students who demanded the right to attend faculty meetings, the new faculty voted, over the opposition of several of us, to make all its meetings open. In this atmosphere of "full partnership" without the familiar security of academic departments, the faculty suffered a peculiar kind of identity crisis from which it never really recovered.

In other ways, however, the faculty asserted its prerogatives. The six social scientists discovered that if they taught all the common social science seminars in the catalog, they could not teach their individual specialties without a heavier load than the humanities teachers. Arguing schedule and workloads, not curricular issues, the faculty resolved to abandon the effort at a common social science curriculum; instead there would be a series of separate electives. This almost happened with the common humanities seminars, but the chairman of that part of the program held the line, partly by not convening the faculty to meet on the subject. He asked everyone for at least one semester to try the proposed reading list (ranging from Sophocles and Plato to Camus and Malcolm X).

On opening night, with their generation's gay indifference to history and prior contracts, a number of the new students protested the agreement the earlier planning staff, including students, had made with the college's local council, a nine-member body appointed by Governor Rockefeller. Though the council agreed that all other social rules could be worked out by the students, it asked that men and women be assigned rooms on separate corridors in the converted stable that was our one dormitory. To applause, one young man charged that the partnership had been betrayed; he wanted the pleasure of seeing girls in his bathroom when he came out of the shower. When the same student used the "betrayal" argument three times during the year, I suggested that only a fool would keep being betrayed all winter long, citing the woman who complained to the judge that, after being raped once, it was just rape, rape, rape all summer long. Another student put the issue in theoretical terms: rigid toilet training and sharp lines between men and women accounted for much misery; an experimental college should try to undo this. At the end of several hours of debate and discussion the students did finally agree to accept this one rule as an unfortunate compromise. But we could not interest them in seeing the relationship between the college and the relatively conservative council or state university officials as an important part of the experiment. For some of us, this was not a liability but a major source of Old Westbury's significance: we were creating not just another independent and isolated experimental college but an integral unit of the largest public university system in the world, which we could hope to influence.

This was *their* college, their experiment, the students said, not the state university's, not Albany's, not the planners'. The agreement in the catalog, which they had read in applying to Old Westbury, was just other people's words; no matter that almost half these people had been students. Later, several students complained to an open meeting of the council that the architectural plans for the first cluster, on which one student planner had worked diligently, should all be redone, though building contracts were already signed, because present students hadn't participated. Chairman Maitland Edey, a supporter of student participation through thick and thin, noted that since it takes several years to produce a building, someone will have to make decisions affecting those who come after.

Caught between these pressures from both faculty and students, I recalled C. Day Lewis's lines: "For where we used to build and love/Is no man's land and only ghosts can live/Between two fires." To me the two fires of faculty power and student power felt much the same, and I feared that the curriculum we had designed was not strong enough or challenging enough to help us break to some new and better ground.

Only with the faculty assembled did I comprehend how deeply ingrained is the resistance to taking responsibility for a coherent curriculum, and how strong is the hold of the academic disciplines into which most standard curriculums are divided. More and more the student platform seemed just a response to—or a caricature of—the established anarchy of every department, every professor doing its or his thing. If we thought we had broken the grip of the elective and departmental system with our first effort at planning a new curriculum, we were sadly mistaken.

Early in the first semester an unusual note was struck by a newly-formed "Nonwhite Caucus" of the fourteen black and Puerto Rican students and three African or Asian students, twenty percent of our eighty-five students. They issued a manifesto calling for courses "such as social organization, statistics, urban planning, languages, sciences and law." Reacting against the white students' emphasis on gentle community and personal growth, they said they could not afford to return to their communities "with merely a 'GG' or 'Grooving in the Grass' degree" but needed "meaningful degrees" representing "the attainment of certain tools" through "hard methodological courses." From this point on the nonwhite students were on balance the main student factor for practicality and academic discipline, tending to want such old-fashioned things as requirements, examinations, grades, a course structure and even teachers. They were the first student group to make any *academic* demands.

On drugs, too, the nonwhite students were a conservative force. Reluctantly, the first student planners had agreed that the politics of survival required Old Westbury to be clean of drugs; it could not afford to be busted as Stonybrook had been. But if it had not been for the black and Puerto Rican students, who at times almost became vigilantes on the issue, many of them having fought hard drugs in their home communities, I doubt that the new students would have carried on the earlier planners' policy. (I am told that the use of drugs on campus varied inversely with feelings about partnership; when students felt they were full participants, even in the midst of confrontation, drugs were down; when the partnership seemed a sham, drug use went up.)

During the year it was hard to be sure whether the program

and partnership were going up or down. Some of the seminars seemed to go very well, others very badly, most were probably mediocre. Socratic dialogue without Socrates is never easy, but the faculty's lack of conviction about seminars and differing approaches added to the confusion. You can call it a seminar, but a lecture by any name is still a lecture or a lecturette. Some saw a seminar as an occasion in which one's expertise is delivered through manipulation of the discussion; others saw it as a bull-session. To develop the understanding and skill to lead a good dialectical seminar the faculty would have to work together over a considerable period of time criticizing and comparing experience and participating in their own seminars. Even our teams of two seminar leaders themselves had trouble sticking together.

"Why begin with *books*?" the students asked in several of the seminars, and in one they prevailed. A psychologist who viewed education as a form of therapy persuaded his faculty partner to agree to the students' proposal that they all spend the next session sculpting in clay on the floor. While sitting under the table, playing with clay, the willing but unconvinced young sociology teacher decided that conventional education was not as bad as he had thought; the next year he returned to his former department at the University of California.

As chairman of independent study, Professor Resnick argued for considerable faculty supervision, criticism and evaluation with students generally required to write a paper on their work, all of which the catalog had promised. But the majority of the faculty supported the student contention that in this third part of the curriculum they should be free to do "at least one-third of their own thing." It may be that in their first year or two in college students would benefit by an opportunity in at least one area to flounder, without getting a failing grade, and perhaps in their frustration discover the need for self-discipline. One faculty member avowed that he would approve anything a student wanted to do, including counting clouds for a semester, though he thought such a horrible example showed lack of respect for the students' intelligence. Many students did excellent work; but the imagination of some in designing exotic projects outran our fears.

"Count on it—if you are a liberal and are sympathetic to the goal of reforming the university, you will begin by pandering to the students," concluded Professor Resnick from his experience. "It is very bad for them because it gives rise to expectations which, later, you will not believe in fulfilling. So my advice is to get it out of your system as quickly as possible. Then you will be able to take students seriously which is what they need and deserve." On this and other issues the faculty became so split that it seemed wise to divide for subsequent years into three curricular programs, which would be the beginnings of our contrasting constituent colleges. Diversification seemed indicated, too, in order to prevent the first program and the students it had attracted from simply replicating itself and shaping the whole college in its image. So, still trying to turn our divisions into a dialogue, Academic Vice President Youtz and I proposed that we divide into separate academic programs for the following year. One program should continue the urban studies emphasis; another would be a disciplines school in which the traditional academic disciplines would be offered, though in fresh combinations and initially focused on the humanities; the third ultimately became a general program with two years of common seminars for those not ready to choose either of the more specialized curricula.

Some faculty and many students opposed this, seeing it as an administrative maneuver to divide and conquer. The living organism we had created, which had been everything, fought against the day when the nucleus would be divided, and when not everyone would be part of everything, when the whole would become greater than the first parts. The faculty voted narrowly to approve a three-fold division, while many students continued their opposition. This was one of the issues in the sit-in by over a third of the first eighty-five students at the end of the year. They demanded the dissolution of the disciplines school, the adoption of a fifty percent quota for "third world peoples" for all jobs and student places, and the establishment of an all-college decision-making system in which each student, teacher, or administrator would have one vote: "Power to the People."

In fact, the power question had dominated more of the year than this account indicates. The first major explosion, just before Christmas, began with the quota demand. A black studies seminar proposed that 50 percent of all student places or faculty and staff positions be reserved for nonwhites. A majority of students adopted this plan and asked the faculty not to deal with the issue as a faculty but to join in deciding it through an all-college assembly with students and staff. In a tense room crowded with students, the faculty finally voted not to submerge itself in an all-college meeting and not to approve a racial quota. This assertion of the faculty's separate identity and authority seemed important and encouraging to me. But the power of the president was also at issue. In the discussions it had been necessary to affirm my readiness to veto a racial quota, which I considered unconstitutional for a public college, and otherwise questionable. The proponents argued that a fifty-fifty racial division would enable race to be forgotten and true integration achieved. We predicted that this would make race a constant factor; we were not prepared to substitute such a dubious experiment for what we saw as our main business—the search for a new curriculum of liberal arts.

Outside observers of that week of many meetings were impressed by the political education underway and the good dialogue, but many idealistic students were frustrated by the defeat of an idea they considered exciting and beautiful. In a simmering mood they left campus the second semester for field assignments in black and Puerto Rican sections of New York.

"Education-in-action, whether in the inner-city ghetto . . . or on the other side of the globe, should leave the actors thirsty for knowledge and theories to make sense of the experience." So we said in our catalog. But the experience of one term in the ghetto left most of our students thirstier for more action. "This college," wrote a group of the students who participated in the sit-in, "should be committed not only to 'understanding' these things but to *doing something about them*." Or, as one seventeen-year-old white girl said on her return from teaching in a black school: "It's not a liberal education I want. I hate liberals. I want an education to be a radical."

Toward the end of the year, Herbert Marcuse visited campus and brought unexpected music to my ears. To student complaints that Old Westbury was a college of, by and for the Establishment, he replied dryly that he had got all of his basic education in the Imperial Gymnasium of the Kaiser's Berlin; they could do it too, if they shunned soft courses and took the hard fundamental ones, if they read major books, studied history. When they challenged the centrality of books or the morality of taking time for theorizing, he held his head in his hands and said:

> You too, like so many in your generation, have a deep intellectual inferiority complex, yet this is a time when anyone who wants to cope with the world has to be more educated, more theoretical, more intellectual than most men have ever been, and if you want to do anything toward bringing revolution of any kind in this world, you will have to be ten times as intellectual. Your resistance to things of the mind is deep-rooted, but deep-rooted though it be, it must be uprooted by love if possible and by force if necessary.

Soon afterward twenty-five or thirty students occupied two of the temporary geodesic domes into which we had moved after the fire. No force was used, no physical damage was done, but the only sign of love was a bottle of Manischewitz wine left on my desk, when—under the threat of our going to court for an injunction—they moved out. This was the demonstration during which one of the lively banners read, "Paranoia is True Perception." The press contrasted this relatively peaceful affair —"Sit-in With a Difference" ran one headline—with bombings and arson going on that very week on nearby campuses.

But for some of us it was about the end of a road. The near tantrum that broke out when Chairman Edey of the College Council and I made it clear that we would not accept even the so-called "moderate" proposal that students constitute fifty percent of all decision-making bodies; the wild threats in the negotiating meeting that led a psychiatrist present to warn a number of us to lock all doors and windows; the vows of the sit-in students to reopen the struggle in the fall; the moral imperialism of the dominant group of activists who treated even students who opposed them as pariahs; the silence of the moderates; the unrepresentative political composition of our little island of idealists (to the discomfort of Republicans being asked to finance our venture, a student leader cheerfully told a university budget hearing that at the college "We're all to the left of Hubert Humphrey"); the sad fact that political turmoil was taking so much time that no one's full creative powers had been really turned to teaching, research or artistry—and our inability to break this vicious circle: all this convinced me and many of my colleagues that a drastic revision was required.

One night, thinking about the surgery that would be needed, I remembered a day on a farm near Selma, Alabama, where I was stationed in the Air Force in 1944. A veterinarian and I were riding horses when we came upon a cow about to die in delivery. My friend had to get ropes up inside around the calf and we had to pull for a long time. The calf is dead, he finally told me, but we have to get it out to save the cow. We did and saved the cow. The first experimental program was dying; we had to try to save the college.

Our diagnosis was shared, more or less, though for opposite reasons, by one of the leaders of the sit-in, who tacked an "EPITAPH" on the bulletin board:

> Old Westbury hasn't just failed. It's dead.
> . . . It was never experimental; it never even attempted to be really different; and it didn't succeed in "keeping us down."
> . . . The whole world was dying, but we hoped Westbury would be different.
> It isn't. Black students demand the right to be middle class: to get a solid "academic" education and a degree that will let them be teachers and social workers and lawyers and councilmen—black American citizens enjoying the fruits of whatever it is that is vital in the American dream. White students oppose the intrusion of the American Way into their do-your-own-thing utopia. Students and faculty rally to the cause of their own self-interests.
> Meanwhile Bobby Seale is gonna hang. There will be one, two, three, many Song My's. A half-million Americans will be marched to Allentown, Pa. And American businessmen will get an "open world."
> Westbury isn't different. We're racist and imperialist and bourgeois—and dead.
> Heil, Hitler!

Phase Three

The transition of these last years to a new Old Westbury was helped, I hope, by my decision in August 1969 to go to Bryn Mawr as soon as a new president could be found. When an alumna on that college's presidential search committee telephoned, I said I had made enough mistakes at Old Westbury to disqualify me forever from further educational leadership. "But haven't you learned a lot?" she asked. The committee hoped the next president would open Bryn Mawr somewhat more to the world but also respect and maintain its academic standards and scholarly tradition. They thought my experience might have made me ready to do just that.

After each encounter with Bryn Mawr's faculty-student-trustee search committee, the appeal of that college's excellent standards, steadfast traditions and serious students grew. What a school for conservatism Old Westbury had been! Some students had been radicalized, at least temporarily (though two parents in Texas were grateful that their son, a Stanford radical who transferred to Old Westbury, had returned much sobered; the poster of Mao remained on his wall, but he went to work for a Senator only a little to the left of Humphrey). For me, however, a curious thing had happened and may tend to happen for the president of an experimental college: the logic of the situation seemed to require the president to play an increasingly conservative role, to check competing demands for scarce resources, to prevent the college from being pulled in a hundred different directions. The last thing anyone wanted at Old Westbury was a new idea from the president. Everyone was having trouble enough dealing with my first ones.

A remark by our daughter rang true; after watching our college-making for three years and then going to Yale as a freshman, Susanne said:

> If only the experiments at Old Westbury could have been tried with students who came to *study*, in a place where the walls were a hundred years old, where the habits of crossing courtyards to class were set, so you didn't always need to worry that with any new idea the whole tent might collapse!

Would Old Westbury collapse if I went to Bryn Mawr? Wasn't it time for that first tent to be collapsed and a new one raised? If so, couldn't a new administration do it more easily and with less resistance? With a clear mandate from the State University, a new president could be given almost the same opportunity I had. The presidential search, which would involve our faculty and students with the council and university trustees, might be the "reality principle" Old Westbury needed. In a State University, for better and worse, power does finally belong to the people—to the people of the state and their representatives.

Machismo said stay and fight, but wasn't it the wrong war in the wrong place? Fighting radicals, libertines and young idealists at Old Westbury was hardly a future to prefer; a new president could best end that war with powers of complete reorganization.

"You Fink!" said a student friend, after the news that I had said "Yes" to Bryn Mawr. Seeing him come around the corner, I remembered his last letter to me, protesting an old story he thought I had used too often: A Negro witness before a congressional committee, when asked which he would choose, the U.S.S.R. or the state of Mississippi, said, "I'll take Pennsylvania."

"You see I really did mean that story," I said. "I'll take Pennsylvania."

From Paris, where (as my secretary noted) all good revolutionaries spend their summer vacation, two of the sit-in students sent this postcard:

> Good news travels fast. We are so happy that a snooty Establishment liberal like you is going to a snooty liberal Establishment place like Bryn Mawr. Now Old Westbury is our dream alone. Don't mess!

At a meeting of new black students, a strong young man asked me: "We hear you are leaving because these white radicals have caused a lot of trouble. Would you change your mind if some of us promised to take care of them?"

He and the other black students did play a key role in reducing political pressures during the transition. Leaving Old Westbury's special program for disadvantaged students, mostly blacks or Puerto Ricans, was part of the pain of going. At a time of increasing racial separatism, this program, including about a fourth of our by then two hundred students, was remarkably well-integrated academically and socially; it was probably the best legacy left to the new administration.

With the shadow of uncertainty over everyone, 1969–70 was an uncomfortable year. The search for a new president went well with the elected faculty-student committee working closely with the council, but it dragged on till late spring. At first the fact of transition was sobering, and the academic programs seemed to be thriving though only about thirty students each had chosen the disciplines school and general program, with the great majority choosing urban studies. Later, as I took some unpopular administrative actions on faculty and staff appointments, designed to give the new president the freest possible hand, there was a resurgence of opposition, and I felt the awkwardness of a lame duck.

Then in the spring came Cambodia and practically everyone's energy turned to opposing the President of the United States, a fact noted with some relief by quite a few college presidents. Though I did not join in the faculty's vote to impeach Mr. Nixon, I helped organize a protest by a number of college and university presidents and approved the faculty's decision not to close the college but to make it an open college for education on the war.

Old Westbury's first graduation, for a number of two-year transfer students, took place on our front lawn on a bright May day. Students had said they wanted no ceremony, just a party. "You mean after all these years I come to my child's graduation and no one even calls her name?" a mother said to me sadly. Agreeing completely, I arranged an impromptu ceremony; Chairman Edey of the council presented them their degrees and I gave each a flower, my last official act.

Looking at the graduates, all of us present—friends and foes —agreed that for most of them the intense experience seemed to have been worthwhile. "We have all earned degrees in college making," said an outstanding student, who has already entered the new profession of educational innovation, discovering that consultants from Old Westbury draw good pay. Quite a few of the first students said they would become college administrators or teachers and practice the educational reforms they had preached.

Had we been too critical of our creation? Had our own expectations, like the students', been too high? Or had we forgotten the powerful education that can come from tragedy? Perhaps tragedy, revolt, and disappointment—and hopefully recognition and understanding—are all built into the history of any experimental college worth the name. After a visit at the depth of our pessimism Kenneth Keniston of Yale, after noting all our complaints, wrote that he had "never seen a college where students were so thoroughly involved with the future of the college." The Middle States accrediting association sent a shrewd critic to appraise our program; on her first visit in 1968, Dean Elizabeth Geen of Goucher College wrote:

> I'm convinced you've got something going that is appropriate to the times—and all times for that matter. I wish I could be one of the students.

A year later, even after seeing how plagued we were with what she called the "Heraclitean flux" of each student generation demanding the right to change the college's erstwhile shape, and after warning that all our programs were neglecting the sequential structure of knowledge, she still said, "You builded better than you knew."

I wish I thought that were true. With more time perhaps we could have made it true. Our field program had just begun to face the problem of converting experience into knowledge. One semester is too short a period for withdrawal and return, the adrenalin of action runs too strong after a short time in the ghetto; but shouldn't we have kept at the problem of finding the right formula for field study, by trial and error? Developing an urban studies program that is a liberal education and not just a new specialty, designing a curriculum that will produce liberal artists instead of either pedants or fools, will not be done without a lot of imagination and long experience.

Another hard question is whether those of us were right who resisted student power and the main student platform of a free-form, "do your thing" curriculum. Our dean of students, Henry Scott, to the end argued that we were wrong; if we had all relaxed and enjoyed it and given participatory democracy as the students defined it, a full chance, he predicted we would have seen politics disappear and creativity blossom.

A sensitive sociologist who headed the urban affairs program, Russell Ellis, was showing some success in this approach, working with our most radical students. With the responsibility of shared power, the wild ones were fading into the woodwork, according to Ellis. And if we have a college with a skewed student body that attracts and serves—saves, might be his word —the range of students from hippie to activist, all to the left of Humphrey, so what? There may be a million like them in need of a place like Old Westbury.

Was it what they needed? Or would they have been better served by a curriculum that challenged them by greater love and force to do the harder things so many of them are avoiding, to cross the greatest cultural frontiers, which are more likely to be found in the library than in the ghetto?

In retrospect, I wish our initial two-year program had concentrated, for example, on Greek and Mathematics, an immersion in the worldview of Fifth Century Athens and in the world of numbers behind modern science and technology. That experiment, a real "outward bound" of the intellect, would surely have taken them by surprise. It might have broken the grip of twentieth century irrationalism. For thoughts like this, a student called me a "stubborn medieval mule."

"You are a tragic hero, and don't take that as a compliment!" a former student and good friend said when I left Old Westbury. "Your blindness is the tragedy. You still don't see and accept where we are." But seeing doesn't mean accepting.

Another student who lived through the early days, one of the first planners, wrote recently that the "shrillness and moral imperialism of our times has troubled me enormously for the past year, as I have found my criticisms and dreads about our society, and particularly about youth, increasing." He wished they had been "more aware of the personal injury we were so easily administering to you. I never really had a sense of how difficult, ambiguous and uncertain your position was. . . . In some ways youth is blind, and it is a winning vulnerability but often a dangerous one."

If we are all somewhat blind, it is not surprising that we were unable to lead each other to places better than where we were. If we are even a little Socratic—let us forget giants—we can take this not as a confession of defeat but as a sign of what we still need to learn. For the wave we called student discontent and hoped to ride into rapid educational reform is clearly part of something bigger, deeper and society-wide that shows no sign of passing. Nor should we want it to pass.

Thanks to Old Westbury I know more clearly how much I stand against part of that current: the iconoclasm, fear of authority, insistence upon relevance, resistence to requirements, refusal to accept history, retreat from the intellect and books to sensitivity and drugs, and the anarchy of everyone "doing his thing." But this is not just a student phenomenon. Point by point it is mirrored by the culture all around us.

How much a college can do to enable people to understand our modern flux and effectively resist it, change it or knowingly join it, I am not at all sure. But more than ever I know I am interested in the "common thing"—the coherent curriculum and Socratic search that would make a college deserve the ancient description, "republic of learning."

A strange, funny, sad story. This account is only a fragment of the many lives we lived in those intense years. The lessons are being applied, one way or another, in many places, including Washington's new Evergreen State College on the edge of the Pacific where our academic vice president, Byron Youtz, along with two other faculty members, have gone with a new opportunity for curricular innovation. Our other vice president, Jerome Ziegler, is now Pennsylvania's Commissioner of Higher Education.

At the new, innovative Hampshire College in Massachusetts, according to their admissions officer, they are trying not to admit too many students with high verbal but low mathematical scores in Scholastic Aptitude tests. They say this disparity, especially in men, indicates great idealism but little realism, and their study of Old Westbury's records convinced them this was our pitfall. We older planners and faculty may also suffer a verbal-mathematics gap; certainly the gap between idea and reality was great.

In May 1971, at the closing ceremony for our first program at Old Westbury, students presented a plaque that read, "In the beginning God created Old Westbury, and it was good." He didn't, and it wasn't. But the three-day "celebrative bang" that drew us back together from all over the country to "mark the end of that marvelously strange and delightfully ambiguous experience" (to quote the invitation) caught more of its spirit, including its pride, than the *post mortems* by observers who look only at the corpse.

Not unlike the graph of American colleges generally, the last year of the program, 1970–71, had gone smoothly, directed by Council Taylor, a popular member of our faculty. It ended, as we had at graduation the year before, with flowers. At Old Westbury, twice is a tradition.

By then the new president, John Maguire, an associate professor of religion and academic innovator at Wesleyan, one-time room-mate and friend of Martin Luther King, Jr. and a 1961 freedom rider in the South, was assembling a new planning staff and developing a new program into which our remaining students and faculty were merged in 1971–72. His initial plans for a quite different student body, older and more locally based, with a large proportion of low-income Long Island residents and an even larger proportion of blacks and Puerto Ricans, for a curriculum built around the theme of human justice and for full partnership—this time with women—are as ambitious as any of ours.

How the new Old Westbury deals with its history and what lessons it draws will be one of its critical tests. A warning from the past: the air on F. Ambrose Clark's beautiful estate has proved intoxicating to all occupants so far. One can already note that the new Old Westbury is in no way more like its predecessor than in its proud determination to be entirely new.

V Fairhaven College

Such a funny little movie I live in with tragedies and comedies and a million other inadequate terms for one enormous thing. But I can't even find a certain set of mind to carry me through it all. I don't think there is such a thing. It's far better to be quietly and amorally overwhelmed. . . .

A FAIRHAVEN STUDENT

DREAMS

From the Fairhaven College Catalog
1971–72

Liberal education is that which is truly relevant to an understanding of the human condition. It is designed to liberate the individual from the restrictions imposed upon him by ignorance, prejudice and provincialism. It helps the individual to understand himself, the people around him, the world around him and to see it all in historical perspective so that he may prepare himself to live in a changing world that is the natural consequence of its history. Liberal education is not directly concerned with making a living or with adjusting the individual to the world as it is—it is preparation for living in a changing world. . . .

The Fairhaven Philosophy

One of the most important aims of the Fairhaven program is the development of individual responsibility. Fairhaven College is an educational program with residence hall living serving as an integral part of the educational experience. Although Fairhaven residence hall government is primarily a matter of student self-government, the rules, regulations and their enforcement are developed by procedures which the college community, students and faculty have worked out together. The educational goal of individual responsibility suggests that there exists a minimal number of living restrictions; this allows maximum opportunity for the individual to assume responsibility for his own life. In turn, students share a responsibility for the college and its success as a whole.

Two basic assumptions underlie the various procedures here mentioned and those established in the future. First, Fairhaven College is an educational environment and consideration for the student as a scholar and his rights to study and interact with others as part of his educational program is of first importance; second, the student is an adult member of society and his individual freedom is supported to the extent that it does not interfere with the rights of others.

REALITIES
Growth by Fire

GARY B. MACDONALD

The author was a student at Fairhaven until he left it in December 1970. He spent a year travelling, living on a farm, and editing this book and is now back in college—though not Fairhaven—pursuing a traditional degree.

1

Fairhaven College is a four-year, liberal arts, residential "cluster" college attached to Western Washington State College (WWSC) in Bellingham, Washington. The designation "cluster" means Fairhaven was chartered by the Washington State legislature to be a small (maximum enrollment 600), semi-autonomous division of WWSC; the parent college grants the Fairhaven degree and provides its services and educational facilities to Fairhaven students. At the same time Fairhaven retains its own faculty and administrative staff and power to set its own academic goals and self-governing procedures. Major changes or innovations in Fairhaven's curricular and social circumstances must be cleared by WWSC's provost or board of trustees, both of whom are regularly apprised of Fairhaven's progress.

The college opened in September 1968 with eleven faculty and a freshman class of approximately 200. The Fairhaven curriculum consisted of a number of required courses in several general academic disciplines. Students were required to complete a "Great Periods" humanities sequence of five courses covering aspects of human history from classical Greece to the present; a science-math sequence with emphasis on the history and philosophy of scientific thought and method; one course on behavioral science; and several elective courses on a wide variety of topics. Also, students were required to demonstrate competency in composition and to complete one to several independent study projects.

The typical Fairhaven classroom approach was the seminar: small, informal, conversational, with few if any lectures and little traditional evaluative criteria employed, such as grades and tests. Rather, student work was evaluated in writing, either satisfactory or unsatisfactory, by Fairhaven faculty, who taught or advised all Fairhaven seminars.

But Fairhaven's total curriculum comprised only about a third of the credits necessary to receive a bachelor's degree from WWSC. So students were expected to select a major and minor from among WWSC's many offerings and to complete these at WWSC.

That first year, because Fairhaven's separate $3.5 million campus had not been completed, the community was housed in a dormitory complex on the WWSC campus. Therefore, it was subject to WWSC's social regulations: dorm doors were locked nightly at midnight and members of the opposite sex were not allowed in private rooms after ten on weeknights, 1:00 A.M. on weekends. Feeling these regulations to be restrictive, a few students researched and analyzed other college's visitation policies and proposed a new Fairhaven policy that allowed virtually unlimited intrasexual visitation. This 24-hour visitation policy passed a community vote of approval in the spring of 1969 and was thereafter put into effect. It has remained unchanged since.

Also in the spring of 1969 a constitutional convention was convened to devise a government for Fairhaven. Up until that time the college's dean had personally appointed committees to handle college operation; he no longer wished to do so. Therefore, two constitutional proposals finally came before the convention. One advocated an "open" committee structure in which students, faculty and administration were given one vote each. Membership on the various committees was to be voluntary. Further, to prove commitment after having volunteered for a committee, a person would have to meet a committee meeting attendance requirement before becoming an official voting member. The other constitutional proposal also granted community members one vote each, but provided that committee membership be determined by election.

By community vote the second proposal, slightly amended to incorporate elements of the first, was ratified. This new constitution created several elected committees: policy board, the main decision making body in the college; two curriculum committees, one to adjudicate requests for elective seminars and a criterion for independent study, and the other to handle required seminars; communications, responsible for making committee minutes public; Fairhaven committee, responsible for dormitory life and allocation of dorm funds; a judiciary board, responsible for disciplinary action according to conditions of due process as outlined in the constitutional document; faculty hiring, tenure and promotion; and admissions. Typical committee membership included a balance of students, faculty and administration each having one vote. In the case that Fairhaven's dean might, as he could, veto some policy made in committee or in the case that a committee itself made an unpopular decision, the constitution also provided a process whereby the Fairhaven community at large could recall the veto or unpopular decision. Except for those considering confidential data, all committee meetings were open to the community.

In 1969–1970, Fairhaven's second year, the college moved from temporary quarters into its own administration and dormitory buildings not far from WWSC's main campus. The change of physical environment was mirrored in curricular changes as well. Early in the year dissatisfaction became apparent with Fairhaven's required curriculum; many students and some faculty were not pleased with either course content or the teaching techniques or even with the whole idea of a required sequence of courses at all. They believed that a greater diversity of nonrequired courses was preferable to a "common intellectual ground," which Fairhaven's required curriculum was supposed to facilitate; the required courses had failed to provide that ground, they argued. Eventually articulate elements in the community won approval for an "area requirements" curriculum. Instead of being required to take specific courses in the humanities, science and behavioral science, under the new curriculum students would fulfill specific *area* requirements. For example twenty credits in humanities, twelve credits in science-math and so on.

Fairhaven seminars had always covered a variety of subtopics under general requirements. Rome, for example, was covered from artistic, architectural, intellectual and governmental angles. Now, however, a flood of seminar titles appeared, some for elective credit and others specifically offered toward fulfillment of one or more area credit requirements. (Also, WWSC course offerings, in certain cases, could fulfill area requirements.) Since few seminars were repeated quarter to quarter, or, for that matter, year to year, it became possible to offer well over one hundred individual seminars in a year's time. Independent study flourished. Though some were dissatisfied with the new curriculum, most of the community seemed to like it. Those in the first freshman class who preferred the required sequence over the new system (because they had already completed several required courses) were given the option to either continue under the old system or transfer credits into the new system.

Among the other major developments during 1969–1970 was an increasing awareness by many that, because Fairhaven was a residential college—students were required to live in college dormitories throughout their undergraduate career—and because, in some cases, campus life was not the most conducive to the best learning situations, Fairhaven should encourage learning experiences off-campus. One of the off-shoots of this awareness was the development of a travel program whereby Fairhaven students could receive credit by engaging in activities of their own choosing outside Fairhaven. Consequently, one faculty member and several students spent spring quarter, 1970, in Mexico, traveling and attending classes at a Mexican university. Plans also began to be made for other structured travel experiences.

During Fairhaven's second year the college housed nearly 400 students. Faculty numbered sixteen.

Fairhaven's third year, 1970–1971, began on a note of tragedy. Charles W. Harwood, dean and one of the early planners of the college, died in a boating accident the night before school opened. His death created an authority vacuum which was quickly filled by a faculty member who left his academic duties to become acting dean.

During this year Fairhaven experienced a predictable attrition of students, many of whom had gone on to more specialized study in other colleges and universities so that enrollment totaled only about 450. Faculty numbered twenty, incorporating professionals in areas such as literature, economics, mathematics, psychology, physics, art, American history, philosophy, political science and music.

Notable innovations also developed in both the social and curricular aspects of Fairhaven life. In the social area a proposal passed the policy board whereby fifty students from the community at large could live off-campus for three quarters if they had already lived on-campus for three. This development freed the college in many respects from having to think of itself as solely residential. It also gave students the opportunity to participate in learning experiences outside Fairhaven for credit toward their degrees.

Another innovation, related to the freeing of Fairhaven from its residential role, was the development of the Fairhaven concentration, or, as it was more often called, the Fairhaven "major." Pressure had been building since the college's inception to create a program in which those students who did not wish to take a major at WWSC could design their own concentration of courses, preferably in a specific area or discipline, directed towards a specific goal. Now it had become possible. Concentrations were to include at least 50 credits as part of a well-integrated, usually interdisciplinary academic goal. Students wishing to design concentrations had first to put together a tentative listing of desired courses or learning experiences and then coordinate a concentration committee of faculty from Fairhaven, WWSC or elsewhere who would advise and evaluate the student's work in the concentration. All of this had to be approved by a Fairhaven faculty coordinator.

This new concentration system made it possible for Fairhaven students to take responsibility for virtually all of their undergraduate career, to move among other colleges and universities at will for specific academic enrichment, especially to put their perceptions of how they were changing and growing into action by revising their original concentration proposal as they progressed toward the degree. Thus, the degree became more meaningful for many students who had previously considered it insignificant. By the end of spring 1971 several students had already begun work on a variety of concentrations.

Also, travel programs became more popular in 1970–1971.

No less than four fully accredited tours led by Fairhaven faculty occurred during the year. One to Mexico again, one to Greece, one to Japan and one to Europe. In addition several students were traveling throughout the year under their own auspices, receiving credit in the bargain. Others were off on other campuses for a quarter's time, doing independent and course work of individual interest.

In the spring of 1971 Kenneth Freeman, former dean of Bensalem College, was selected by a specially formed committee of students, faculty and administration to be Fairhaven's new dean.

The college's fourth year, 1971–1972, began with an enrollment close to 550 and a faculty of twenty-three. Joining the faculty were a former practising lawyer, a Far Eastern history scholar, and a skilled outdoorsman who has since resigned.

Further innovations in curricular structure occurred. A new academic program was ratified by Fairhaven's faculty for testing during winter quarter, 1972, in which most Fairhaven seminars were only of two-week duration. While students were able to take quarter-long seminars (the traditional length of classes), many could choose from among several "mini-seminars" on a wide variety of much-narrowed subjects. With this new program it was possible for a student to enroll in several more intensive classes than he would normally be able to take in a quarter's time. Especially since winter quarter was divided into five two-week sessions, it was also possible for students to take a regular credit load and a two-week vacation besides. Several faculty have already suggested that it become the standard winter program at Fairhaven.

Also during 1971–1972 travel programs in Washington, D.C., Chicago, Mexico, Ireland and Greece were planned.

One hundred Fairhaven students lived off-campus, as opposed to the fifty maximum of the year before. Fairhaven has since dropped its residential requirement altogether.

Thus, with this brief history, we begin to see how Fairhaven College has grown. From its beginnings with a structured, required curriculum, Fairhaven has initiated new curricular innovations which now, in many ways, make the college an educational "clearinghouse": students may come and go as they please, using Fairhaven as a temporary base of operations while they glean personal direction from its rich curricular offerings and also take advantage of a faculty which increasingly regards itself as resource-oriented. When direction is found, students may pursue their goals in a variety of ways, either at Fairhaven or elsewhere, for Fairhaven credit An infinite number of possible combinations of courses, seminars, independent projects and travel programs exist from which an equally infinite number of different, truly tailored degrees could result.

From its beginnings in a fairly structured, residential social environment, the college has expanded to become a community one sixth of which lives off-campus, a fifth of which is traveling in the United States or abroad at any given time, and one hundred percent of which is no longer restricted by repressive dorm hours and impractical bed checks.

But of course no environment as diverse and provocative as Fairhaven's admits of simply one story. There are other ways to tell the tale.

2

When I graduated from high school in 1968, I cared about nothing except arriving at some arrangement with my environment that would allow me time to reflect on both my history and potential. Public school and my previous experiences had taught me to distrust perceptions of my capabilities. I was not emotionally equipped to make autonomous decisions. A horrible inertia pervaded all my activities and thoughts, even though

I always kept up the illusion that I was above vacillation. Clearly, any solution of what to do with myself after high school would be accidental.

Fairhaven College was the accident. I happened to hear of Fairhaven from a friend, who, while singing this new "experimental" college's praises, added that it needed boys for its first freshman class. I hurriedly applied, was accepted and enrolled all within a very short time. The decision involved little forethought and no expectations. Yet college, *any* college, was not a completely accidental next step after high school. Public school instilled in me the awesome expectation that all good American middle-class children go to college. It was logical that the one expediency, public schooling, should be followed by another, college. Also, my home background contributed heavily to the pressure. So, even had I been capable, let alone willing, to consider other alternatives than college after high school, the odds were securely in favor of my speedy matriculation in the nearest academy.

So it is possible to establish accident as the primary cause of at least one student's enrollment in Fairhaven. Whether or not my "methods" for choosing Fairhaven, and my subsequent good fortune at having made the "right decision" after all, applied to the other 200-plus Fairhaven freshmen that autumn of 1968, however, is still a question deserving analytical survey. Though most of us denied the presence of sheer chance in our decisions to attend an untried new college, I suspect that I had many more soul-brothers than I cared to imagine, which probably describes one aspect of the mood with which we began to create our learning alternative in Fairhaven.

We did not know what we wanted. We knew only what we did not want, but even the infrequent ability to agree on what was undesirable would cause a series of upheavals in our fragile community.

We were fragile because we were part of a new and decidedly

different college. Compared to any other college in the state of Washington in 1968 and also to the vast majority of American collegiate institutions in general, Fairhaven had all the makings for an academic rebellion. The idea was to create a small intellectual environment conducive to close faculty-student relationships and devoid of the pressures and inane traditions that rape real learning on huge, impersonal campuses. Also central to this notion was Fairhaven's "living-learning" experiment, which encouraged adult behavior on the part of students by subjecting them to few all-college regulations. The assumption was that, by allowing them this leeway, students would come up with behavior modes among themselves conducive to a comfortable living environment and continued intellectual growth. Actually, it was necessary to make such an assumption under the circumstances because Fairhaven was, by definition, a residential college.

To the extent that they supported these ideals, the original Fairhaven faculty was a euphoric, dedicated lot. One remembers a brilliant Scots hotshot in literature who delighted classes with his acidic wit and clever philosophizing; an unassuming MIT graduate in physics who mortified pubescent freaks with class questions like, "Do you masturbate?" and "How would you describe the analogy between sexual climax and intellectual perception?"; the artist who entranced audiences with tales of his gambling exploits on the French Riviera; the wild-haired opera singer (with a Ph.D.) whose fondest dream was to build a harpsichord from scratch; a grand old patriarch of psychology; and a kind Scandinavian with a passion for Wallace Stevens.

The first freshman class (subsequent freshmen seemed more talented) also cut a distinguished figure in Fairhaven's design. We were for the most part Caucasian city-dwellers who had come from reasonably affluent backgrounds. Two-thirds of us had graduated in the top quarter of our high school class, half in the top ten percent. Half had belonged to honor societies, a fifth garnered National Merit recognition, and more than a third had been elected president of some high school organization. One hundred percent thought students should design their own curriculum (which was nice because that was largely what Fairhaven proposed to let us do), though a third thought the individual could not change society. Half had no religious affiliation whatsoever, nor did two-thirds have any stated idea of what they would do in life. And 87 percent of us, as compared to the 25 percent national average for college freshmen the same year, thought marijuana should be legalized.

Other, subsequent surveys found Fairhaven's general student population to be bright but impractical; personally conservative, opposed to making changes in themselves, yet politically radical; enlightened, but often prudish. It was the beginning of a continuing list of paradoxes and ironies that would color everything we tried to accomplish and render a good deal of our agonies and growth-pains absurd from the start.

But, at the start Fairhaven life was calm, occasionally even methodical. I steeped myself in Greek literature, history and philosophy; the philosophy of religions; oriental literature and religion; introductions to drama and fiction; the writers of the "lost generation"; the philosophy and history of science; human sexual behavior; excursions into the poetry of Stevens, Eliot, Whitman, Crane and cummings and experimental and progressive education; and a junket editing and designing Fairhaven's first literary magazine. And I began to change. I took to wearing exotic, funky clothes. Hair grew everywhere, and the jargon of the age became my jargon. Ideas leapt out to be touched, taken or ditched in an endless discovery. The world got suddenly larger and I somehow smaller, lost in its contours. For the first time in my short history I began to run the high risk of being what I sensed I really was.

But I was soon to discover that the manifestations of hip—

liberating one's body, language and mouthed ideals—do not create a liberated individual. Certainly not in my case and hardly ever in anybody else's case. To a human as naïve and trusting as I was then, the difference in behavior between what people said and did, what they thought and how they acted, especially among the young, can be a hard-knocks education. In my case that education to the hard realities of Fairhaven life, the people who lived and worked there, was, for a time, simply shattering.

Sometime during that winter of 1969, while stoned senseless (for the first time) on hash, I was slipped a hit of acid by a companion. It was not a bad trip in itself, but the fact that a friend could take it upon himself to provide me with such a potent mind-bender without being certain I really wanted to take it, took a long time for me to reconcile. Certainly this one experience made me suspicious of the motives of Fairhaven's dope freaks and of nearly everybody else's motives too.

As it turned out suspicion was not an altogether bad approach to Fairhaven life after all. Not that Fairhaven was necessarily worse than any other academic milieu; on the contrary, in some ways it was better than most. But for those who cared to penetrate the college's beatific façade, there was much to dislike about the place.

First, allowing for the fact that the college had just opened and was therefore disorganized, many Fairhaven seminars were, in my opinion, inferior to classes I had taken in high school; some were simply awful. This was true largely because students and faculty alike were unwilling to prepare for the intensity of intellectual dialogue and carry it past the conventional lecture format. One also remembers too many seminars in which the discourse, if ever started, was petty, wholly emotional or otherwise unsatisfying. (If the Fairhaven admissions committee had ostensibly accepted only those it considered capable of disciplined work, then something had gone wrong;

even the most enlightened among us seemed unable to leave
behind their egos when they came to class. Learning was not
a matter of quest, discovery and further quest but of "I happen
to know more than you do, I'm sure.") Of course, these things
happen on campuses everywhere, but poor-quality classes were
being called "experimental" and "innovative" at Fairhaven.
Perhaps many of us harbored too-high expectations of what
college level work would be like after all? However, it is not too
much to hope that small seminars and intimate faculty-student
contact generate *some* academic spark.

In any case I was disappointed in much of Fairhaven's general
curriculum. Most of the academic work I have already described as my own was, in fact, independent, not classwork.
After three quarters of frustrating Fairhaven seminars, *all* of
my work was independent. Only after a moratorium on seminars for more than a year did I try one on Norman Mailer and
the study of American politics since World War II. The seminar
promised to " . . . examine American politics from the perspective of realities, fiction and nonfiction." But the professor, a
political scientist, "did not feel capable" of handling the relationship between Mailer's political sensibility and artistic temperament, a crucial relationship. Thus, all of Mailer's fiction
would not be included in class discussions, nor would that portion of his nonfiction which spoke of artistic goals and their
effect on his work be included. Why, then, did the professor
offer the class? I dropped it immediately, and thereafter avoided what had become a painfully typical Fairhaven seminar.

Actually, independent study worked well for me, probably
better than most classes ever could because I like the challenge
of being on my own. In fact subjective estimates indicated that
everybody was doing some sort of independent work and enjoying it more, in most cases, than their classes. This may not have
been because everybody thought poorly of Fairhaven seminars,
for, by itself, independent study can be exciting learning.

But there were drawbacks to so many students engaging in independent study. This became more apparent when, in Fairhaven's second year, its formally required curriculum was changed to a series of area requirements, which facilitated even more independent work. Although many private projects make for enormous academic diversity within a college community, they can splinter the intellectual base and continuity upon which any college of the liberal arts builds.

"Common intellectual ground" was often mentioned as one of the goals of Fairhaven's original required curriculum of particular humanities, science-math and social science courses. Yet the great popularity of independent projects, coupled with increasing lack of interest in required courses (which resulted in the change to area requirements), made for very little in common to talk about. In varying degrees everyone was keeping a lonely vigil with himself, crossing and recrossing intellectual turf that was alien to others. Thus, learning at Fairhaven, rather than being a definitively social process, was becoming an individual exercise—an anxious and lonely evolution.

Finally, this evolution in Fairhaven from group to individual learning, while for many a welcome change, was, for most, an isolating experience. Most of us felt stranded because we had never been called upon to do disciplined independent work and did not know how to begin. Further, in many cases we lacked adequate support from both peers and faculty to *want* to become independent learners and almost always lacked even the minimal direction necessary to know *where* to begin. So we perambulated about the horizons of available knowledge, vaguely aware that we were missing a lot and habitually unaware that missing anything made any difference.

Second among Fairhaven's questionable aspects was its faculty.

I have often, in all seriousness, compared myself as a forthright Aries to what collectively must be the faculty's Cancer sun sign in the astrological zodiac. Actually, astrology states the case rather well, for Cancer will never, unless provoked, approach a problem directly. The crab (Cancer's correspondent in the natural world) dances nimbly around its prey—in the faculty's case, concrete decisions about anything—until that prey shows intentions of disappearing, at which point the crab grabs and will not let go.

One often found oneself relying on the stars for guidance when an issue came before Fairhaven's faculty. As a group they seemed remarkably impervious to opposition, suggestion and even, emotion. Recently, I witnessed their delay and finally abandonment of a crucial question: Fairhaven's academic direction, its goals and needs. Conversation on this important topic took four hours, was often gifted, even cogent, but it was indecisive to a fault. At least the faculty was consistent; their efforts to arrive at a concensus have been indecisive since the college opened.

Not that each professor does not have his and her merits. In fact each of them is prepared to handle a number of intellectual pursuits and, with fluctuating success, does so. The majority are personally likeable. But it seems that since many of them left traditional departments to join the nondepartmental faculty at Fairhaven, they have been confronted with a peculiar identity crisis: their validity as teachers in the absence of classes and the secure, definitive support of a department. Some are solitary, lonely creatures in spite of their colleague's friendly companionship within Fairhaven. An observation often made is that Fairhaven's faculty individually enjoys less contact with professional peers than the lowliest lecturer in the hugest university department might. Thus, lines of interacademic communication, sustenance and growth break down. Quite possibly in hot pursuit of solutions to this nagging personal dilemma, many of Fairhaven's professors have felt incapable of confronting the validity of themselves as a faculty in general.

As a group they have neglected Fairhaven's ragged social milieu; procrastinated the problem of how to grant credits for independent and travel projects—important aspects of the college's academic dynamic; and, most critically, ignored the cohesion of all of their classes and seminars into an integrated, interdisciplinary Fairhaven curriculum.

When the faculty and the curriculum are at loose ends so is the school. At least this has been my own contention since 1969, as I wrote the faculty a series of three open letters over a period of two years, the gist of which was that students were dissatisfied with classes (for reasons I have already outlined), that the faculty was largely ignoring its potentially stabilizing role in the community by not displaying more initiative and resolve as a group, and that, finally, if the faculty did not heighten its awareness of all aspects of Fairhaven life—not simply the academic—the school would doubtless continue along its uprooted path. Predictably, all of the letters were ignored, or perhaps a kinder word is disregarded. One professor saw fit to correct one letter's grammar and syntax, but that was the extent of the response.

It is wrong to place *all* of one's hopes in one group of men and women contained within a community of many more people all of whom share responsibility for the community's future. Yet one insistent demand of all Fairhaven community members was that they remain cognizant of their relative importance in Fairhaven's gestalt. Because the college ostensibly exists to educate, one can hardly underestimate the importance of the faculty's responsibility in this respect. Nor, on the other hand, can Fairhaven's faculty afford to disavow the existence of certain elements in the gestalt but not others; the faculty, as everyone, is obliged to inspect Fairhaven's totality, not just selected constituent parts of that totality.

Another important requirement of the Fairhaven faculty is that, in addition to their intellectual competence, they must function as a role model. The faculty in general seems to feel incapable of, or opposed to, projecting their personalities as images for behavior guidance among their students. Yet this is largely what Fairhaven students need them to do. Neither does it do the faculty any good to pooh-pooh their importance as role models; in most cases each of them was hired and retained (by students on hiring and tenure committees) with precisely this criterion in mind. Thus, the faculty is trapped into leading too-public lives; their life styles, thoughts, and dreams are not their own. This overwhelming publicity of motive and action probably accounts for the faculty's tendency to leave Fairhaven's premises at every opportunity, to go home and try to lead calm, private lives. And it also accounts, on the other hand, for many of their zealous, sometimes painfully superficial, commitments to various Fairhaven *causes célèbres.* When professors are not trying to escape their students, they are trying to join them in a cause, and vice versa, or both simultaneously—a kind of schizophrenia that may have become *de rigeur* in the Fairhaven environment.

Third, and perhaps most prominent complaint about Fairhaven is its fractured social milieu in terms of dorm life and interpersonal relationships. In both instances, Fairhaven social life fluctuates between subtle crisis and disaster. Middle ground is rarely achieved.

Begin with drugs, the inevitable (but generally least important) area of concern. Of course, most people at Fairhaven turn on, or have, with a variety of concoctions. However, from the beginning most Fairhaven students have been cool about dope, booze or whatever. Only isolated cases of drug abuse stand out, but these have given Fairhaven a reputation as an "opium den" of sorts that is wholly unwarranted.

In 1968–1969 before drugs or the drug cult had consumed us first freshmen, our dope freaks were an oddity. They had an almost hallowed status in the Fairhaven community. Their stories of acid trips, mescaline highs and so on evoked awe more often than disgust. But these stories, in fact the entire drug cult aura, *did* evoke disgust in some quarters, and here is where I think the real problem with drugs in Fairhaven began. Ultimately it was not a problem of drugs at all but of how drugs were used to manipulate sentiment and the psychological impact of the cult created to sustain the popularity of drugs among the young. In short, the problem was between "straight" and "hip."

It was a subtle cold war between the two factions. However, the effects of the war were obvious.

Everybody in the community was classified by his peers as either "hip" or "straight." When the straights classified a person as "hip" it meant that he or she used drugs or lied about using them for purposes of ingratiation, engaged in "free fucking" for its own sake, had adopted the hipster lingo for all occasions, expressed avid devotion to the Movement, peace, and love and decried the wretched state of the Union, parents, "pigs" in general, the Vietnamese war and, *carte blanche,* everything else not adherring to the ethic. "Spontaneity" was at a premium, even if that behavior was immature or destructive. Anyone who hinted that something besides hip existed in the world was suspect.

Most suspect were the "straights," who, according to the hip, were too dedicated to studying, hard work, the traditional ethics of self-reliance and conservative individualism, frugality of behavior (called "tight-ass" by the hip), and had a condescending attitude toward all those who did not believe and behave likewise. The hip, on the other hand, often regarded as straight those in their own ranks who, even though they smoked dope and so on, held out for linear concepts of communication, thought, and behavior.

In the behavior that we inflicted on one another we were all cruel children. Paying far less attention to our similar needs than to our apparent differences, we reinforced wretched behavior and attitudes in one another with gusto. I suppose it is impossible for one human being to *help* another in the sense of changing him by coercion. But it is definitely possible for one to abstain from providing another with incentives for self-destruction (mostly mental, but physical as well). Sadly, however, we provided those incentives among ourselves. We "offed" everything and everybody, went on mad drug and booze binges, lost several members to various mental institutions, others to extended vacations on acid, still others to self-induced hermitage in locked dorm rooms. Fairhaven's physical environment became disposable: lounge furniture was destroyed, dogs and other animals ran wild through our dormitories. And I will never forget a young woman who astonished me one morning as she sat reading *Reader's Digest* in the library, when she said: "Man, I try to experience every kind of pain I can. Pain is truth." Her sentiment did not seem unpopular; pain was Fairhaven's truth.

The pressure young people feel to go to college coupled with their lack of confidence and emotional maturity, the lack of direction in the curriculum, the absence of role model support and leadership from faculty and other adults and the hostilities of the social environment—all of these combined to make Fairhaven an education by fire. And those who grew, grew by fire as well.

Needless to say, the sparks flew. I was perhaps closer to these sparks than most because, for a year and a half, I was a confrere at Fairhaven. Translated from the French to mean "brother," a confrere is actually nothing of the kind. When I held it, the position was one of resident disciplinarian within a particular Fairhaven dormitory of fifty people, but more often than disciplinarian, counselor to the unsettled and upset.

From the beginning Fairhaven has had a peculiar internal disciplinary system, administered by the confreres (Fairhaven students selected by their peers and faculty) and their superiors the adjuvants (older graduate students selected by the same process, who also lived in the dorms). That system was called "the informal procedures"—a gross understatement to be sure. Basically, because Fairhaven had so few social regulations to enforce, little besides infractions of the public peace, violations of local, state and federal laws pertaining to drugs and firearms and various roommate hassles ever came to the resident staff's (confreres and adjuvants) attention for disciplinary action. When such infractions did occur, however, they were dealt with in the following manner: First the confrere talked to the culprit(s). If this was ineffective up to three conversations about the same, repeated violation, then the adjuvant stepped in with harsher admonitions. If he could not help, the case went to the assistant dean for student affairs at Fairhaven, an administrator who oversaw the resident staff. Then the student's faculty tutor took over. If all of this failed, the infraction finally resulted in an official case before Fairhaven's judiciary board, composed of elected students, faculty and administration. The board is empowered by Fairhaven's constitution to mete out various "punishments," the worst of which is permanent expulsion.

It was an ineffectual system borne of Fairhaven's equally ineffectual insistance on a residential requirement. Students in general had no intention of obeying common rights "guidelines." They sidestepped all of them with impunity, knowing that the resident staff, who were anxious not to alienate, and, besides, could not themselves get a handle on the meaning of their jobs, would probably do nothing anyway. The students assessed the disciplinary situation at Fairhaven correctly.

Of the several major cases that deserved judiciary attention which occurred between 1968 and 1971 in Fairhaven's dorms, only two ever reached the board. The second, involving drug usage in a private dorm room, was made a mockery of by a slick Seattle lawyer hired by the defendants. Though hiring a lawyer was certainly sanctioned in Fairhaven's constitution, one strongly suspects that the college never expected it to happen. The entire case was discreetly dismissed for lack of evidence, and the validity of the judiciary board, as well as that of the entire disciplinary system, was thereafter up for grabs.

However, complaints from resident staff and community alike about the ineffectiveness of the disciplinary system obscured the fact that, in counseling situations with fellow students, the staff achieved commendable success. A spate of suicide attempts, drug freak-outs, personality adjustments and growth-pains were effectively handled in private sessions with confreres, adjuvants and the assistant dean for student affairs. In fact the counseling end of the staff's job, as I recall it, was rewarding and enlightening, though rough emotionally. The students themselves also benefited from the staff's conciliatory presence in the dorms, though they might not admit it.

With the death of the residential requirement in 1972 and the realization that the effectiveness of confreres and adjuvants as disciplinarians was also on the wane, things changed at Fairhaven. For the past year by official direction from the assistant dean, the staff has not policed the dorms but devoted all of its time to counseling and crisis situations. And there is a proposal before the community (sure to be accepted) which would abolish the present staff altogether, replacing them with a "living faculty" of four professionals in psychology, project and systems development, craftmaking and first aid/medical services, who would all live on-campus and center their collective attention on creating a 24-hour crisis clinic. All of these areas have been seen to be real needs of the Fairhaven community which no unskilled staff can adequately handle.

In any event the dorm environment at Fairhaven was volatile. One witnessed so much plain stupidity, anguish and self-destruction that after a while, out of exhaustion, one was effectively reduced to wondering why it had to happen at all. As a confrere I became in many ways unswervingly conservative and cynical (quite a switch from my hip days), for too often the same people who complained about their neighbors in disciplinary matters stood up and fought in their behalf—on "philosophical" or "ideological" grounds—when the neighbors were called on the carpet. This happened too often for comfort and made for unpleasant scenes between people who might otherwise have been able to work out agreeable compromises.

In this chaotic hot-bed of discontent it was odd that Fairhaven's government enjoyed a higher degree of success than other aspects of the community. At least so it seems to me. Allowing for manifestations of the social polyglot I have already described, government committees seemed to carry on business with few setbacks. It may be inferred from this that an order imposed *on* chaos almost inevitably creates some order *out of* chaos.

On the other hand the fact that Fairhaven has an orderly government does not mean those it affects will energetically participate in it. On the contrary it now seems as though the great initial enthusiasm invested in Fairhaven's first constitutional convention in 1969 has fallen off; interest in government has come to be expressed mainly in private dissatisfactions with this or that aspect of the committee structure, not in actual committee membership. This may be a result of general student weariness with revolts and protests, not to mention governments, in general. Yet it would also seem that if we were tired of the fight, we would try other methods to cure our ills and dissatisfactions. Such is apparently not true at Fairhaven. Not that government committees want for members—they do not. But members of committees have tended to be the same people, who often simply shift from committee to committee until they have made the rounds, while the larger student body has remained apathetic, except when it is sniping.

Like every other position of authority at Fairhaven (and there are not many), the dean's is ambiguous. The ambiguity of his position, however, is unlike that of other positions. For the dean alone must walk a taut rope between WWSC's administration, to which he is ultimately responsible, and the Fairhaven community.

Often the administration at WWSC and the Fairhaven community seem to be mutually exclusive elements of the same process, yet it is notable that so far Fairhaven has gotten everything it wanted. The progenitor of these innovations in community life has not always, if ever, been the dean. Yet without the balm of respect he carries with him into WWSC's provost's office or trustee boardroom, ideas that have been given life would likely have died quickly.

When it is not ranting about one thing or another, Fairhaven is usually nit-picking. No better example exists of this truism than the laborious check-and-balance safeguards placed upon the selection of a new dean for Fairhaven after the previous one died. I know. I chaired the committee that developed the criteria with which another, separate committee could finally proceed to solicit a new dean. In the first constitutional convention some of us merely distrusted the dean; in these committees to select a new one, we got around to distrusting each other; more precisely, we *began* by distrusting one another, distrust being another near-truism of Fairhaven life that probably finds it origins as far back as the haggling between straight and hip.

In the deanship committee I chaired, we argued the matter of authority at Fairhaven into oblivion. At one point, so bent were we on eliminating the dean's office altogether (and so ignorant of the political exigencies which necessitate its existence) that we called in four other academic deans from WWSC, ostensibly to "tell us what it is like to be a dean; what *do* deans do?" Our guests effectively snapped us back into the realities of a state-operated higher education system of which Fairhaven is of course only one small part. Without a dean, the deans assured us, Fairhaven would be in real trouble. A further suggestion from some of us, of a triumvirate of deans for Fairhaven, tickled their hard-nosed approach to administration. The provost and board of trustees needed *one* man to whom they could look for information and assurance. Traditional, static responses? Of course. But that taut rope the Fairhaven dean walks is anchored at either end by tradition and stasis; the system to which he is responsible is still largely traditional; and, the Fairhaven community is itself temperamentally tradition-bound, looking and reacting to the past much more often than it casts an eye to the future.

Under the circumstances the deanship committee decided finally that candidates should be sought who would remain loyal to Fairhaven, no matter what the coercion from WWSC may be. Naturally. But as usual this decision was not made without at least a modicum of blood drawn.

3

Any over-view of Fairhaven is necessarily subjective as the evidence accumulated to this point must indicate. Indeed, one of the often overlooked joys of the community was that everyone in it had a distinct personal notion of what was happening because everyone experienced Fairhaven in a different way. However, this multiplicity of potential insights into the workings of the college, rather than contributing to a constructive diversity of opinion, generally worked *against* Fairhaven. Nobody really got together on a consensus view of Fairhaven's goals and potential future. Thus, Fairhaven has been aimless, which might be some sort of peculiar virtue if aimlessness did not hurt so many people.

Yet Fairhaven has always been aimless. Even in the beginning, it had no goals as an institution save for a few philosophical flourishes about the ideal liberal arts education and ideal students and faculty. This is true largely because in 1966, when planners first began to devise this new academic creature, a good deal of incredibly romantic dreaming went on with little if any wise forethought about the future. The planners—members of WWSC's faculty and administration—hoped to "create an atmosphere (in Fairhaven) conducive to experimentation with curricula, teaching procedures, staffing arrangements, independent study and the use of new educational technology." (This and following quotations are from "A Plan for Fairhaven College," dated 1966.) To accomplish this end they endeavored to hire a faculty who had "scholarly interests and competence that extend the boundaries of any single discipline," who had displayed a "willingness to experiment with new curricula and new instructional procedures," and who had a "willingness to work closely with students." Potential Fairhaven students would have to "evidence . . . the kind of maturity and self-discipline required for independent study and participation in educational planning," and exhibit a "potential to become adults *who will make substantial contributions to mankind after graduation.*" (Italics mine.) Together, then, the students and faculty would work in the beginning with "broad interdisciplinary courses based upon great ideas, great books, geographic regions or historical eras." There was also provision for "extended . . . independent study" and "student-led seminars which may at times meet with no faculty member present." But "since the required basic curriculum is to be determined by the Fairhaven faculty, after consultation with Fairhaven students, the form which this will take cannot be predicted in detail until the faculty has been selected. . . ."

On the question of the residential aspect of the proposed Fairhaven community, the planners were equally ambiguous but firm. "It is hoped," they wrote, "that students will [live in the dormitories] because the use of residential facilities to enhance the student's educational opportunities is an essential part of the plan." What about those students who did not wish to live in the dormitories? "There is ample room for them in other programs . . ." Thus, Fairhaven's residential *requirement*.

Astonishingly, the document which contains these at best vague proclamations is the *only* definite statement of Fairhaven's goals ever in existence. Even today such heady hopes have not been fleshed out in any concrete way, although literally reams have been written either in philosophical support of or opposition to them. Some of us are justifiably amazed therefore, that in the context of this nebulousness the college has survived as long as it has.

But that is not all; everybody seemed to want to get into Fairhaven's act. None other than WWSC's president in 1966 decided on the physical characteristics of the new college's dormitories. He thought it fitting to reject flatly an originally modular, one-building plan (which, looking back, was worlds finer than the archaic dormitories finally built on Fairhaven's multi-million dollar campus) in favor of a cherished fraternity model: twelve dorms housing fifty students each; each dorm, it was doubtlessly assumed, wanting to be a separate entity unto itself, eating in separate dining rooms (twelve of which were incorporated into the administration building), and perhaps even having its own colors and so on. Further, students who now wonder why their single and double rooms are the size of monastery cells do not have far to look. Cost estimates for the Fairhaven campus were figured on total square footage; the president's twelve dining rooms ultimately eliminated space to breath in private rooms.

So it was in this atmosphere of bungling interference and inept planning that Fairhaven College found its genesis. That the profound changes enacted over four years upon an originally vague set of guidelines have been chaotic goes without saying. But here is a point: even though those guidelines *were* vague, the Fairhaven community since 1968 has had the opportunity to seize the moment and create a viable, integrated, innovative academic program. In most respects it has not bothered to do so. Even when Fairhaven has made changes in its academic and social environment, these have invariably been enacted piecemeal regardless of how each innovation relates to and affects others. No attempt has been made to correlate the various aspects of the community into a comprehensive picture of Fairhaven which might shed light on its present gestalt and point possible directions for the future.

This does not mean that innovative developments do not continue to be made within the community. On the contrary, as evidenced by the two-week "mini-seminars" being tested as this is written, the business of creating alternatives is alive and well at Fairhaven. But, will anyone attempt to relate "mini-seminars" in terms of importance and effect to Fairhaven's curriculum in general, its improvement and further definition? Likely not. Or, to make the argument more historical, did anyone really understand the implications of changing Fairhaven's required curriculum to area requirements; of changing its social environment by implementing 24-hour visitation; of liberalizing the off-campus allowances and introducing the Fairhaven concentration; of encouraging students to travel; even of abolishing Fairhaven's residential requirement? A few have always reflected on these considerations, but their occasional wisdom, borne of experience and survival in the college itself, has never seemed relevant to a community like Fairhaven's which is bent on destroying its own fragile history as it races forward into—into what? Where? How? Nobody really knows.

Why this pell-mell, know-nothing charge into tomorrow? Even had Fairhaven's planners put together a cogent, particularized program in the first place, much of what is wrong with Fairhaven is wrong with the age in which we live. The zeitgeist of our present culture—its characteristics correctly identified by Alvin Toffler in *Future Shock* as being transience, diversity, and novelty—will not allow the romantic ideal of a small, cloistered, Oxford-style college to exist for long. America today will certainly not allow such an ideal to succeed for it no longer provides for the real needs of contemporary students. There is no use chiding Fairhaven for being unable to resist those problematic conditions which no one could possibly have planned for in 1966. As one of Fairhaven's founders now sadly concludes: "Had our plans been made for intelligent kids in the mid-fifties Fairhaven could have worked as we hoped it would. As it was, we had no way to predict the ways in which the needs of young people would change so completely in such a short period of time (1966–1968)."

What are the real needs of young people in college today? Time. Time, as they say, "to get themselves together"—an awesome, tough task in most cases because the present generation did not grow up in an environment which encouraged introspection and self-knowledge; they did not learn to discipline themselves or to be capable of autonomous decision making, which is required before they will be satisfied by a Fairhaven-like program, and indeed before such a program can succeed at all. Confronting oneself is a frightening, repercussive event worthy of much greater attention than it is now getting. To cope in a positive way with the rapid rate of change in our present society, an emotionally and intellectually integrated personality is not only preferable, it is essential and at a comparatively earlier age. The life-dynamic in which one has forty years to live before he finds it necessary to tie up loose ends no longer suffices. The age demands that we be all-together *now*.

Besides time to figure out who and what they are, students need an educational environment which provides challenging, free learning situations in which they make their own choices as well as institutional leverage allowing unhassled completion of self-chosen goals.

Students also need colleges and universities that, while facilitating challenging learning experiences, are also simultaneously committed to helping students in their own self-discovery. Self-development services and programs of an implicitly psycho-sociological nature are essential as means toward this end.

Because students' intellectual competence often far outstrips their emotional maturity, all academies of higher learning must begin to articulate with concrete programs the essential relationship between intellectual competence *and* emotional maturity as the two central facets of a true liberal arts education. Institutions must stop simply paying lip service to the ideal juxtaposition of one to the other and then "hope for the best." Without institutional help the best cannot often happen.

If these are real needs of today's students, then an apt question is whether or not America's higher education system is *the* Institution to deal with all of them. Of course, I must answer no. Students might often find the emotional growth situations they need outside of higher education: in travel, work or whatever. Yet I would also point out that, if current literature detailing the breakdown of the traditional institutions of home and church which in the past have been responsible for providing maturing experiences for youth is valid, then America's schools and colleges are logically (by default) the next institutions up the social ladder to bear these abandoned familial and religious responsibilities. That America's vast education system has made few meaningful strides to date in dealing with this new role is common knowledge. That the system's survival in the future may ultimately depend upon its dealing in some way effectively with such responsibilities is not.

Attempting to *ensure* that students fit some preconceived

(and mostly ridiculous) notion of fine, upstanding young adults when they graduate from college—a proscriptive process known in the past as *in loco parentis* in which the institution polices the behavior of its students—has gotten American colleges and universities in general into a good deal of trouble over recent years. But, by *facilitating* emotional growth, academies of higher learning could take greater advantage of contemporary group dynamics, counseling, T-groups, "sensitivity" and human growth workshop processes, which can enormously compliment strictly intellective learning. Actually, such processes (though they sometimes alienate more than integrate potential growth) can enhance the human dimensions of what is only grasped abstractly in great books and great ideas.

Ironically, in its present state Fairhaven provides at least the possibility of satisfying all of these needs. Its curriculum, no matter how recklessly created, provides the possibility of free, choice-oriented educational opportunities so badly needed by today's students. Its almost completly unrestrained social environment, no matter how poorly constituted, provides the possibility of life-style variety needed by young people to determine how they want to live and what makes them unique personalities. In short Fairhaven students already live in an environment which grants them the space to grow up.

But, as I have implied in other sections of this essay, most Fairhaven students do not take advantage of this space. Because they are generally incapable of providing their own direction, students are caught in the breech of Fairhaven's unrealized ability to create a sound interdisciplinary education. Perhaps the principle offenders in Fairhaven's lack of self-direction are its faculty, who have continuously begged the issue of the college's educational goals with great eloquence but little professional integrity. The faculty must therefore realize that it is they who suffer from their own lack of integrity, as well as the students. And at Fairhaven, without being snapped out of their inertia with a hammer-blow from committed professors, the students are suffering as they squander their kinetic, creative energy on the kinds of destructive behavior I have described. Without direction, all growth must be growth by fire.

So it seems that in Fairhaven we have swung away from obligatory, punitive education towards the extreme opposite sort, which is often so nondirected, nebulous, and nihilistic that it is not an education at all, but a kind of slaughter with good intentions. We have gone from ignoring to overcompensating ideals—and each modus operandi has failed. What we need is adequate middle ground, such as I have suggested—a structured interdisciplinary curriculum where faculty and community talents would combine in an ordered fashion and where students would be at ease with themselves and their surroundings. Such a curriculum would provide students with a base from which to proceed, yet not stifle their commendable urge to experiment.

Saul Bellow wrote:

> . . . this liberation into individuality has not been a great success. For a historian of great interest, but for one aware of the suffering it is appalling. Hearts that get no real wage, souls that find no nourishment. Falsehoods, unlimited. Desire, unlimited. Possibility, unlimited. . . . But one notices most a dramatic derivation from models, together with the repudiation of models.

Not very hopeful. But the conclusion to this same quotation might just as well apply to Fairhaven's future:

> The spirit feels cheated, outraged, defiled, corrupted, fragmented, injured. Still it knows what it knows, and the knowledge cannot be gotten rid of. The spirit knows that its growth is the real aim of existence. . . .

Bellow concludes that "Perhaps the best is to have some order within oneself. Better than what many call love. Perhaps it *is* love."

It is here, in ourselves, that we must first begin to make revolutions—otherwise the Fairhavens in this world only perpetuate our inert social pain.

Meditation
GARY B. MACDONALD

The book is its own best spokesman. There seem to be no real
conclusions to come to regarding what these stories about five
experimental colleges have to tell. There are only the stories,
and whatever they suggest about the process of creating educational alternatives, about the problems seemingly inherent
within substantially free academic and social situations and,
finally, about what might be done with experiments like ours if
they fail and what can be learned from mistakes.

Bacon's hourglass seems an appropriate figure to describe
that part of the American experimental college movement
represented in this book. It suggests movement and time, especially time, and a certain finiteness as well. Beginning as far
back as the early sixties, it began to be obvious that higher
education in the United States was in trouble. The system as a
whole was growing into a colossus, thus becoming impersonal,
if not wholly obnoxious to human life. Gifted men and women
responded to the problems by putting together all of their
dreams and making out of them concrete proposals for alternatives to the educational status quo. All of which was relatively

simple, given the prevailing mood of excellence and superachievement in all fields in the sixties with special emphasis on dabbling in the avant-garde. Some of these proposals, finally, were accepted and even subsidized by existing larger colleges and universities or state higher education systems.

But from each of their inceptions the colleges fell on hard times, all of them for internal reasons and a few for external reasons as well. What are the reasons? The list might read like a primer to controversial facets of the late twentieth century: demands for more freedom from both students and faculty; demands for student power from students; demands for conformity and respectability from financing banks and insurance companies; demands for this, demands for that and very little satisfaction with even the minimal academic freedom to innovate granted all five colleges. Experimental college life was a maelstrom into which all, the naïve and wise alike, fell headlong. Yet while a maelstrom can challenge, it is certainly not the peaceful lagoon so many probably expected. In fact, as we recall from the introduction to this book, "Given the imperative of freedom, people will not be satisfied," whether those not satisfied were people within the colleges or people in the observing societal community. Then we must ask: with what exactly would everyone be satisfied? And here, finally, we come to the central fact in experimental education today, which is that there is no way under heaven to satisfy everyone educationally, even though all of our five colleges tried—how they tried! However, a possible conclusion is evident: in the trying is the salvation. It is the beauty and anguish of trying to provide an alternative to bad higher education (an alternative that may never become a totally successful reality) that mitigates all the pain and provides impetus for trying again if the first attempts fail. We may have to face the fact that within the mass of people on Earth today it may never be possible to educate as we would like or as we think people *ought* to be educated. And yet we must, it seems, keep laboring to do so.

So the hourglass is turned over and begins sifting its sands again. Antioch-Putney seems alive and well, if a bit troubled by internal power struggles. Bensalem, at last hearing, is fated to undergo major surgery in the hands of parent Fordham University, becoming at last a mere shadow of its former raucous self, if it survives at all. Fairhaven's prospects for longevity appear doubtful; enrollment has fallen off and money is scarce. Franconia has a new president and is open again for business, hoping that the New Hampshire countryside is by this late date ready to cope with inevitable outrageous behavior from its students and staff, and that banks and insurance companies may come to see the importance of being unconventional. And Old Westbury sports a new head administrator and a new academic program designed to promulgate a little more inner stability and, it is prayed, happiness as well.

Roy P. Fairfield is now with Union Graduate School and enjoying it. Judy Scotnicki is in Washington, D.C., working. Elizabeth Sewell has "gone underground," as she puts it, teaching at Hunter College in Manhattan. Kenneth Freeman is at Fairhaven, and Rose Calabretta writes that she has work to do in the Dominican Republic. Richard R. Ruopp is now employed with an educational consulting firm in Cambridge, Massachusetts, and we have no news as to the whereabouts of his colleague John Jerome. Finally, Harris Wofford is at Bryn Mawr in Pennsylvania.

So the sand sifts, and what can be said? That academic freedom invites too many romantic, unconventional people to its hearth, and that these are prone to vexatious extremes of behavior? That extreme behavior makes for uncomfortable academic environments or no academic environments at all? That the absence of an academic atmosphere (defined perhaps as a private and interpersonal, but above all, peaceful pursuit of knowledge and wisdom) *in the midst* of what is being called an academic atmosphere makes for embarrassing moments when it comes time to explain to trustees, taxpayers, parents and financial backers what exactly is going on? That the entire question of what is freedom, and what is not, in an educational circumstance is a question still up for grabs, still undefined? That a truly viable alternative within the system to traditional American higher education has yet to emerge on a significant scale? And that, finally, anyhow, our five alternative experimental colleges have given us some insight into what is possible between people and institutions, and what is not or doesn't seem to be? Yes to all of them. Yet that affirmative, and the questions it answers, are all one person's opinion. There are countless other opinions, too, as many as there are people in experimental programs across the land. And the manner in which the questions are asked intends no irreverence towards what happened or is happening right now in those experimental programs because the questions are asked out of remembrance of much sadness and growth.

Leave it to others some years from now to look back on what we have to say here, to concoct studies, to analyze all of it, and to come up with definitive answers. But let it be remembered, too, that definitive studies of the ills of American higher education are what gave rise to Antioch-Putney, Bensalem, Fairhaven, Franconia, and Old Westbury. Remembering this, let us hope, as Eliot did, that

> The end of all our exploring
> Will be to arrive where we started
> And know the place for the first time.

Selected and Annotated Bibliography

FRANK JAMES

Editor's note—Mr. James, a friend, former roommate and student of Fairhaven College, was kind enough to put together the following bibliography. Very much concerned with the present condition of and future possibilities for education, especially radical and innovative education, Frank has personally read all of the items which he includes below. Many of the titles in this bibliography are not generally known: that is, not published by major houses or widely advertised. But the material is excellent, certainly in large part controversial.

This bibliography is divided into three parts: Core, Context and Bibliographies. The Core items were chosen because they are timely and important discussions of key problems for education, and higher education in particular. Each item either analyzes the current status of a major problem or develops a plan for concrete changes in education. Context items were chosen because they provide background material about current problems even though they do not directly discuss the central problems of the Core items. The Bibliographies section is devoted to a review of some of the major efforts to create educational bibliographies, some annotated and some not, for those who wish to delve further. Another consideration in selecting the sixty-eight items was that they be current and generally available to the public.

CORE

Books

Becker, Howard S., et al., *Making the Grade: The Academic Side of College Life.* New York: John Wiley & Sons, 1968.

Remember John Dewey? his philosophy (along with G.H. Mead's and William James's) forms the basis of a sociological perspective called symbolic interactionism. Dewey, via interactionism and Howard S. Becker, is back in education. This book is a report on a several-year study on the function of grading in a major university. The conclusions of the study were that faculty, given their goals, would be better off if grades were abolished and that students ideally would achieve their goals more readily if the grading system were differentiated according to the type of student (the good, bad, and average). Overall they do not *recommend* changing the present system, because the recommendations of disinterested sociologists are seldom followed, but they do *predict* that it will change as a result of interactions between the various interests. Their basic finding is that grading as it now exists interferes with the best interests of nearly all those involved in the educational process.

Berg, Ivar, *Education and Jobs: The Great Training Robbery.* New York: Praeger (published for the Center for Urban Research), 1970.

Berg presents the results of a well-developed, long-term sociological study of the relationship between education and employment. As the title implies, there isn't any; many employes are overeducated and worker productivity does not vary with formal education.

Berman, Susan, *The Underground Guide to the College of Your Choice*. New York: New American Library (Signet), 1971.

Despite the somewhat contrived hip language, seemingly aimed at seniors in high school, this book serves as a contemporary guide to how over 200 major colleges and universities look from the student perspective.

Gaff, Jerry, et al., *The Cluster College*. San Francisco: Jossey-Bass, 1970 (text edited).

Many experimental colleges are "cluster colleges," i.e. subdivisions of larger institutions. Gaff's book reviews all the data (primarily psychological) that has been collected on the cluster college student. Interestingly, there is an amazing similarity in the scores of the students on personality tests (OPI) and in their economic backgrounds (above average). Fairhaven College at Western Washington State College (discussed earlier in this book), and many other cluster-experimental colleges are mentioned.

Freire, Paulo, *Pedagogy of the Oppressed*. New York: Herder and Herder, 1970. (Freire has several other notable publications in English: *Cultural Action: A Dialectical Analysis*, and two articles, one in the May and one in the August issue of *Harvard Educational Review*.)

This book is the unique mixture of two traditions: European philosophy (Hegel, Husserl, Sartre) and radical politics (Mao,

Marcuse, Marx and Engels, Che Guevara). These two lines of thought meet at the common point of Freire's experience as an educator with the peasants of Brazil and Chile. The book revolves around the concept of *concientizacao* (conscientization) or "learning to perceive social, political and economic contradictions and to take action against the oppressive elements of reality." This fits neatly with his definition of education—to become critically aware of your real life situation and to become able to act on it in your own true best interest. Pedagogically he contrasts the "banking" system of education with the problem-solving or dialogical method, the former being widely employed and oppressive and the latter being the true work of a teacher and liberating.

Illich, Ivan, *Deschooling Society*. New York: Harper & Row, 1971. (Illich has also written several other volumes which discuss the basic theme of deschooling: *The Celebration of Awareness, The Breakdown of Schools*, CIDOC Cuaderno #1016, and has written articles for *Saturday Review, The New York Times, The Center Occasional Paper*, and the *New York Review of Books*.)

Illich distinguishes between schooling and education; schooling does more than educate—it has come to take the place of the church and the family in the socialization of children (it is the place where they learn our society's rules) as well as being the social role selector (through credentialing it controls who gets what jobs). Illich maintains that the democratization of education cannot be accomplished through the institution of schooling. The demand for education and its costs are rising faster than national incomes throughout the world.

Illich sees the only solution as "deschooling." The first step in this process would be gaining constitutional protection against discrimination on the basis of prior schooling and legal protection from obligatory, graded curriculums. And secondly, the creation of skill networks, peer-matching services and other alternative institutions, as well as developing a new method for funding education. The redistribution of educational resources is accomplished by a credit card approach which would function somewhat like voucher plans, to insure equal distribution of educational resources. The thrust of all his writing is to return the freedom and the responsibility of education to the individual.

Jencks, C. and Reisman, D., *The Academic Revolution.* New York: Doubleday, 1968–69.

The most comprehensive view of American higher education since Nevitt Sanford's *The American College: A Psychological and Social Interpretation of the Higher Learning.* Topically it covers social stratification, religious colleges, black colleges, coeducation, community colleges, public/private controversy, professional schools, graduate schools, and more. One of its more interesting conclusions is that students are generally in school to get a degree (to be certified) and not to get an "education." The book ends with an excellent collection of references.

Jerome, Judson, *Culture Out of Anarchy: The Reconstruction of American Higher Learning.* New York: Herder and Herder, 1970.

Rochdale, Bensalem, College of the Potomac, Friends' World College, the State University of New York at Old Westbury, and Jerome's own Antioch-Columbia are all reviewed. He deals not only with these specific experimental colleges but also with the general issues of the meaning of degrees, the nature of general education and what he sees as the goals and needs of today's students. (Editor's Note—Not generally a useful book, as compared to the others here. Rather bleeding-heart account of the nastinesses of American higher education, and too many pages of meaningless groping, valid, perhaps, if only they were not pretentious. Good work, however, in the "day-in-the-life-of-a-professor-at-an-experimental-college" genre, and incisive pieces about the six above-mentioned colleges. Reading the book leads one to confirm the belief that college professors, as the graffiti said on the men's room wall, should be obscene and not hurt.)

Perry, W.G., *Forms of Intellectual and Ethical Development in the College Years.* New York: Holt, Rinehart and Winston, 1970, (text edited).

Intellectual development is not possible beyond a certain point without commensurate ethical development. This general theme is explored in terms of the psychological development research done by Perry. He concludes that the two are inextricably interrelated (see Keniston below).

Reimer, Everet, *School is Dead: Alternatives in Education.* New York: Doubleday, 1971.

The compliment to Illich's book *Deschooling Society* (see above). Illich and Reimer have done the same research, indeed, both books are the outcome of a thirteen-year-long dialogue between the two men. Illich's version reflects his European aristocratic background in its style and content; Reimer's version, likewise, reflects his academic background in economics and his interest in political change. It is essentially the same argument for deschooling but from a different perspective.

Silberman, Charles, *Crisis in the Classroom: The Remaking of American Education.* New York: Random House, 1970.

Schools at all levels offer a banal and trivial curriculum, operate on the assumption of distrust and are preoccupied with order and control—these are some of the conclusions of Silberman's investigation. These conclusions are based on a three-and-a-half-year study commissioned by the Carnegie Corporation. It involved a thorough review of the literature, extensive interviews and correspondence with educators and critics, as well as first hand investigation of over 250 schools. Silberman concludes that we ought to shift to a more open "informal education."

Taylor, Harold, *How to Change Colleges: Notes on Radical Reform.* New York: Holt, Rinehart and Winston, 1971. (Other books by Taylor: *Students Without Teachers, On Education and Freedom*).

Similar to *The Soft Revolution* by Postman and Weingartner in that it gives practical suggestions about how to achieve change. Taylor's book analyzes the need for radical reform in the universities and discusses specific things that are wrong.

Theobald, Robert (ed.), *Dialogue on Education.* Columbus, Ohio: Charles E. Merrill, 1967.

A collection of essays on the need to humanize higher education, with an emphasis on interpersonal communication techniques.

Theobald, Robert and Scott, Jean, *Tegs 1994.* Chicago: Swallow Press, 1971.

A futuristic novel in both content and format. It is mimeographed with wide margins in which to write comments; the authors encourage readers to send them their suggestions, to make the book a more and more accurate "history" of the future. Some of the societal and educational changes pre-

dicted are: universities will no longer exist (as they become
more radical the legislatures and alumni become more reac-
tionary); in their place will be problem-possibility institutes
which are living groups dedicated to finding solutions to a
specific problem; another predicted development is a system
which consists of personal two-way communication that is
instantaneous, which is seen as the beginning of the communications era.

Windham, D.M., *Education, Equality, and Income Distribution.* Lexington, Mass.: D.C. Heath, 1970.

The conclusion of this study of the Florida college system is
that the poor would be better off without any higher education. From the point of view of economics the poor pay more
for higher education than they get back from it. (*See also*
article by Hansen and Weisbrod, below.)

Articles

Hansen, W.L. and Weisbrod, B.A. *Journal of Human Resources,*
IV, no. 2, 1969.

Poor families are taxed to send the children of rich families
to college in the state of California. This is based on a study
which utilized a cost-benefit analysis in relation to expendi-
ture of educational resources. The fact is very well docu-
mented with complete statistical breakdowns.

Keniston, Kenneth, "Youth: A New Stage of Life." *The American Scholar,* Autumn 1970.

Reviews Lawrence Kolberg (below) and W.G. Perry (above)
and others to conclude that a "new" stage of development is

coming to exist: youth. This stage of life has defining characteristics in intellectual, moral, and cognitive growth which
can be recognized and measured. Keniston even hazards to
estimate that this new development involves approximately
40 percent of college-age youth. He further seeks to explain
youth's refusal to become part of mainstream society in terms
of this development.

Kolberg, Lawrence and Kramer, Richard, "Continuities and
Discontinuities in Childhood and Adult Moral Development." *Human Development,* XII:93–120, 1969.

Review of current research by Kolberg, et al, which challenges the traditional assumption that moral development
stops with adolescence.

Wolfe, Alan, "The Experimental College: The Noble Contradiction." *Change,* March–April 1970.

Points out the basic contradiction between the democratic
ideals which experimentation might help meet and the opposite direction of all existing experimental colleges, where "experimental" means smaller classes, independent study individually directed by a professor, highly selective
acceptance policies or in the case of private colleges prohibi-
tive expense. Wolfe divides experimenting colleges into several categories to facilitate this discussion.

Monographs

Harman, Willis, "Context for Education in the Seventies." Stanford Research Institute: Educational Policy Research Center,

Menlo Park, California 94025. December 1969. 18 pp. (*See also* Harman's other SRI/EPRC publications)

Harman sees three forces pushing toward a drastic shift in cultural values and basic premises: the existence of a world macroproblem which would require such a shift for its solution, the "Great Refusal" of youth to go along with the values of the past, the questioning within science as to whether its "value free" stance was either appropriate or in the long run wholesome. (Editor's Note—An indispensable essay: well written and wise.)

Nadanjo, Claudio, "The Unfolding of Man." EPRC–6747–3 research memorandum. Stanford Research Institute; Educational Policy Research Center (as above). March 1969. 115 pp.

Survey of over 150 educational methods or systems ranging from gestalt therapy to Zazen. From the historical to the contemporary this survey has a global perspective. Much of its material comes from religious and psychotherapeutic techniques.

Ziegler, W.L., "An Approach to the Future-Perspective in American Education." Syracuse, N. Y.: Educational Policy Research Center, Syracuse University Research Corporation, 1206 Harrison Street, Syracuse, New York 13210. May 1970. 103 pp.

A review of the ways in which educational planning in the U.S. is viewed and an exploration of the problems which the future-perspectives pose for policy, planning, and the educational policy.

Periodicals (Special Issues)

"The Embattled University," *Daedalus*, Winter 1970.

Essentially an effort to explain what happened to the universities in the sixties and to look ahead to what may come. Articles are by Clarke Kerr, Edgar Z. Friedenberger, Erik H. Erikson, and seven others.

"The Future of Black Colleges," *Daedalus*, Summer 1971.

Discusses questions of financing, curriculum, organization, purpose. Basic purpose according to its editor is to make the black colleges a little less "invisible."

"Higher Education and the Poor." *Social Policy*, May/June 1971.

Mostly concerned with the development of the junior or community colleges. Their creation is seen as a method of maintaining inequality rather than democratizing education. Articles are by Frank Riessman, A.M. Cohen, William Birenbum, Paapas and Stern, and Alan Wolfe.

"Revolution on Campus." *The American Scholar*, Autumn, 1969.

Women, black studies, SDS, protest-strikes are the issues covered by authors J. Bronowski, Daniel P. Moynihan, Margaret Mead, and others.

Court Cases

Hobsen v. *Hansen*, 1967. Discussion appears in 81 *Harvard Law Review* 1511 (1968) and 20 *Stanford Law Review* 1249 (1968).

The court held on constitutional grounds that tracking, a system of ability-grouping, had to be ended in the District of Columbia because it prevented equal opportunity in education.

Griggs, et al v. *Duke Power Co.* Discussion by Ivan Illich in the *New York Times*, "Abolishing Schools:" I & II, 71.05.03. p35M; 17.05.04. p45M. Reprinted in *The Breakdown of Schools* by Ivan Illich, CIDOC Cuaderno #1016, 1971. CIDOC, Box 479, Cuernavaca, Mexico.

A unanimous court held that the requirements of a high school diploma or of success in a standardized general-education examination, as a condition of employment, are prohibited under certain conditions by the Civil Rights Act of 1964.

CONTEXT
Early Education

Because of the great number of excellent books and articles in this category, only eight items have been selected for annotation. Others are: *The Lives of Children*, George Dennison; *Our Children Are Dying*, Nat Hentoff; *The Way It Spozed To Be*, James Herndon; *Death At An Early Age*,

Johnathan Kozol; *Education and Income: Inequalities of Opportunities in Our Public Schools*, Patricia Sexton.

Coleman, J.S. et al., *Equality of Educational Opportunity* (The Coleman Report). HEW, Office of Education. U.S. Printing Office, 1966. (Section I, a summary, is issued separately as OE-38000). See also Christopher Jencks, "A Reappraisal of the Most Controversial Education Document of Our Time," *The New York Times Magazine.* August 10, 1969.

Originally this document was intended to assess the effect of segregation on the quality of education. The major expectation before the report was that black schools would be shown to be inferior because of segregation; this was not found to be true. But an even more interesting fact was revealed by the data: that performance in schooling could best be predicted using the parent's income as an index independent of innate ability or "intelligence."

Gross, Ronald and Gross, Beatrice, *Radical School Reform.* New York: Simon and Schuster, 1969.

An anthology which brings together the thoughts of John Holt, Herbert Kohl, Ashton-Warner, and others (see Mac-Cracken, below)

Holt, John, *What Do I Do Monday?*, *How Children Fail*, *How Children Learn.* New York: Pitman, 1967–71. (*The Underachieving School* is a collection of his periodical writings.)

Holt has great insight into the learning process. His anecdotes would be useful to any classroom teacher. It would be unfair to criticize his earlier work because many of its flaws were later corrected. Throughout his work Holt stresses the need for the child to have freedom in education and emphasizes the importance of letting the learner determine the direction of what he is to learn. *What Do I Do Monday?* has a useful list of references, films, and periodicals. (Editor's Note—For the interested but uninformed reader who wants to know why American grade schools are bad for children, *How Children Fail* is a revelation: an excellent book. Holt has worked primarily with grade-school-age children and knows them in the educational circumstance as perhaps nobody else does. The summary to the book is a superb general statement of the reasons experimental education is necessary.)

Kohl, Herbert, *The Open Classroom*. New York: Viking, 1969.

In contrast to Kohl's first book, *36 Children*, this is a manual rather than a description, but the message is still the same— schools can work, if you work at it. In *The Open Classroom* Kohl emphasizes learning rather than teaching. He presents teaching methods and survival techniques for the public school teacher who is willing to try opening up his classroom to innovation.

MacCracken, Samuel, "Quackery in the Classroom." *Commentary*, June 1970.

What starts out as a simple review of *Radical School Reform*, edited by Gross and Gross, ends up a discussion of several of the works of Holt, Dennison's *The Lives of Children*, and Postman and Weingarten's work (see below). MacCracken comes down especially hard on Holt, maintaining that he may be a good teacher but he will probably never be a scholar.

Piaget, Jean, *The Science of Teaching and the Psychology of the Child*. New York: Grossman, 1970.

One of these selections is totally new, the other quite old—both are classics, the conclusions of a giant. If you want to know about child development look to Piaget; he is perhaps the oldest and most prolific writer in the field.

Postman and Weingarten, *Teaching as a Subversive Activity* Delacorte, 1969. *The Soft Revolution.* New York: Dell, 1971.

The former a handbook for teachers, the latter a handbook for students on how to change schools. Both are oriented toward dealing with the practical problems of both groups.

Current Cultural Context

One of the most interesting books in this area is Revel's *Without Marx or Jesus.* Traditionally European intellectuals have maintained that change must come in opposition to the U.S. Revel maintains that change must come from within the U.S. or everyone else loses cataclysmically. See also *The Age of Discontinuity* by Peter Drucker; *The Temporary Society* by Warren G. Bennis and Philip E. Slater; *The Meaning of the Twentieth Century: The Great Transition* by Kenneth Boulding.

Ferkiss, Victor, *Technological Man: The Myth and the Reality.* New York: George Braziller, 1969.

Ferkiss examines the interplay between the social order and technology and concludes that long-range planning will be necessary to avoid ecological breakdown. Not only is planning for industry necessary, but social planning will also be an intricate part of the future.

Ellul, Jacques, *The Technological Society*. New York: Random House (Vintage), 1964.

Ellul coined the term "technological society" which is used so widely today. His book, which unfortunately reflects his theology in its pessimism, is still the most comprehensive analysis of the effects of technology on our society. Although his analysis is still the best, his pessimism has been challenged by many authors. He argues that technology has become an independent force in itself which is no longer controllable. Most of his critics observe that we have certainly gone a long way in that direction but that it is not yet too late to reverse the trend. A special section of the book evaluates technology's effect upon education.

Galbraith, J.K., *The New Industrial State*. New York: New American Library (Signet), 1968.

There is a special section on education with a discussion of how recent social, technological, and economic changes have affected it. Galbraith maintains that control of our economy has shifted from those who own the major sources of production to those with the skill and information to run it. This change has occurred mostly because of the increased complexity of economics and the growing amount of information and training necessary to plan ahead well enough and far enough to anticipate future needs and conditions.

Harman, Willis, "The New Copernican Revolution." *Stanford Today,* Winter 1969.

The most significant aspect of our era, as seen by the future, will be the development of the science of subjective experience. We are in the process of making the next great step in our evolution. Synthesizes the thought of Platt, Boulding, de Chardin, Huxley, and others into a coherent discussion of our present possibilities.

Huxley, Aldous, *Island.* New York: Harper & Row, 1962.

A novel which starts slowly but before it ends discusses some significant problems facing us for the future: overpopulation, overconsumption, political repression, drug experiences and their meaning, as well as the possibility of utopia.

Mead, Margaret, *Culture and Commitment: A Study of the Generation Gap.* New York: Doubleday, 1970.

Dr. Mead argues that cultural systems are changing radically, and that the knowledge of the past is no longer a useful guide to the future.

Mumford, Lewis, *The Pentagon of Power: The Myth of the Machine.* New York: Harcourt, Brace, Jovanovitch, 1970.

In the tradition of Mumford's more than twenty other books, this volume maintains that man and not the machine has been dominant in history. The drama begins and ends outside of human experience but without human experience there is nothing; the machine (technology and its parts-physical existence) is only the dead part of the "action"—only the setting and not the action itself.

Olson, Philip (ed.), *America As a Mass Society.* New York: Free Press, 1963.

Contributors include Fromm, Goodman, Herberg, Mills, Mumford, Riesman, and many more. The book deals with how America is changing in terms of its communities and how people come to have identities. One of the most interesting contributions is Olson's own which surveys a school system whose major emphasis was on creating individuals; he concluded that the pressures for conformity and obedience were overwhelming in their effect on the children.

Reich, Charles, *The Greening of America*. New York: Bantam, 1970.

Reich develops the categories of Consciousness I, II, and III, which represent the extent of development of various portions of the population. He envisions change coming from youth's acceptance of "ecstatic community" in which everyone does his own thing and everyone else lets him do it.

Roszak, Theodore, *The Making of a Counter Culture*. New York: Doubleday (Anchor), 1969.

Traces the development of the "counter culture" from its beat beginnings to the present with excursions to discuss drugs and dissent. It has an excellent notes/bibliography section. (Editor's Note—That's not all that's excellent. I read Roszak's book when it first came out, have reread it two or three times since then, and continue to find it an abidingly fine, level-headed, occasionally euphoric minor masterpiece on hip culture among the young in the United States. Roszak was among the first to take sides, which is to say among the first to pick out the deeper, more profound elements of youthful dissent in the late sixties, and to celebrate the possibility of a better future if only we could tolerate and try to understand the bizarre behavior of some. An excellent, thoughtful tract against drugs is included, as well as a good analysis of the effect that men like Marcuse and Brown have had on the Movement. Roszak is essential reading.)

Theobald, Robert, *Alternative Futures for America II* (Second edition). Chicago: Swallow Press, 1970.

This is a collection of Theobald's speeches and minor writings put together by a group of college students. It contains an annotated bibliography of books, publications, places, and people who are doing important work on the future of America.

Toffler, Alvin, *Future Shock*. New York: Bantam, 1970.

The basic thesis is that we are going through a period in which change happens so fast that we experience the equivalent of culture shock in our own society. The book's shortcoming is that it doesn't develop its thesis as fully as possible; but it remains important because it defines the problems.

Educational Psychology and Human Development

See also Perry, Kolberg, Keniston, in the Core section above, and *Person to Person* by Rogers and Stevens, *The Divided Self* and *Self and Others* by R.D. Laing, *The Art of Loving* by Eric Fromm, *The Authentic Teacher* and *The Self* by Clark Moustakas. For the behaviorist perspective see *Science and Human Behavior* by B.F. Skinner or *Behavior Modification* by Bandura. These are suggested with some reservation: I recommend the reading of Abraham Maslow's *The Psychology of Science* which discusses his disenchantment with behaviorism and his alternative to it.

Erikson, Erik, *Childhood and Society* (Second edition). New York: Norton, 1963; *Identity: Youth and Crisis*. New York: Norton, 1968.

The books discuss development and the problems of adolescence. Erikson deals with both from the point of view of Freudian psychoanalytic categories.

Furth, Hans, *Piaget for Teachers*. Englewood Cliffs, N.J.: Prentice Hall, 1970.

Applies the insights of Piaget to the classroom.

Maslow, Abraham, *The Psychology of Being*. New York: Van Nostrand, 1962.

A classic, the book is Maslow's most comprehensive. It discusses self-actualization, motivation, peak-experiences, and a psychology of health. In small print in the last four pages of the book Maslow lists the "Eupsychian Network" which is a list of all the people, places, and publications of those working on developing human potential.

Piaget, Jean, *Six Psychological Studies*. New York: Random House (Vintage), 1968.

Piaget reviews his most recent work in child development. Each study deals with a specific aspect of development. This could serve as a good introduction to Piaget's work.

Rosenthal, R., *Experimenter Effects in Behavioral Research*. New York: Appleton-Century-Crofts, 1966.

Along with the Coleman Report and Rosenthal et al in *Pigmalion in the Classroom*, this book proves that one of the major reasons for student achievement in school is teacher expectation. When teachers are told students are intelligent, they treat them accordingly and the students come out doing better than those the teachers think are comparatively unintelligent.

Rogers, Carl, *Freedom to Learn.* Columbus, Ohio: Charles E. Merrill, 1969.

The author points out that teachers aren't conventional and boring out of their desire to hurt others. He gives suggestions as to where and how improvements could be made and devotes special attention to graduate education.

Classics

Dewey, John, *The School and Society.* Chicago: University of Chicago Press, 1915; *Democracy and Education.* New York: Free Press, 1966.

Though often quoted, Dewey is seldom understood. His writings are still among the best for insights into the educational process.

Emerson, R.W., *Emerson on Education: Selections* (edited by H.W. Jones). New York: Teachers College Press, 1966.

Emerson's thought and writing anticipated much of what is being discussed today.

Goodman, Paul, *Compulsory Mis-education and the Community of Scholars.* New York: Random House (Vintage), 1970.

Goodman thinks of education as one of the main institutions contributing to a bad society. He is suggesting, although in a somewhat undeveloped form, the alternatives and analyses so popular today. He was the forerunner of Illich in his radical structural solutions.

Huxley, Aldous, *The Perennial Philosophy*. New York: Harper & Row, (Colophon), 1944, 1971.

When Harman (above) sent his recommendations for a "context for education in the seventies" to the House General Subcommittee on Education, this was one of the twelve items he suggested they read. The book is a synthesis of men's thinking over the ages and throughout the world. In the final analysis it must be called a book about religion but its importance for all aspects of life, including education, cannot be overlooked.

Krishnamurti, J., *Education and the Significance of Life*. New York: Harper & Row, 1953.

In this book an Easterner looks at the West: a book about freedom, love, understanding, and the meaning of life. It advises that one be truly free and aware of his motivations before becoming a "teacher."

Montessori, Maria, *The Montessori Method*. New York: Schoken, 1964.

Montessori is still ahead of her time. In her work she has created a systematic method for facilitating cognitive development. Critics point out the obvious shortcoming of this prescribed curriculum method as being too much controlled by the teacher and not enough by the learner.

Niell, A.S., *Summerhill.* New York: Hart, 1960.

Niell develops his educational philosophy and describes his school in England after which the book is named. This is one of the books that has inspired many people regarding innovative education. One of the most important aspects of education as seen by Niell is extensive freedom for children. His writings have given rise to several other books about Summerhill, notably *Summerhill: For and Against* edited by H.H. Hart.

Tolstoy, Leo, *Tolstoy on Education* (translated by Leo Weiner). Chicago: University of Chicago Press, 1967.

In describing the schools he started over a hundred years ago, Tolstoy states a philosophy and describes a school not unlike a free school of today.

BIBLIOGRAPHIES

Marien, Michael, *Essential Reading for the Future of Education: A Selected and Critically Annotated Bibliography.* Syracuse, N.Y.: Educational Policy Research Center, Syracuse University Research Corporation, 1206 Harrison Street, Syracuse, New York 13210. September 1970. 146 items. (New edition of 1,000 items, summer 1971.)

Tiered into three sections according to Marien's assessment of importance. Excellent annotations broken down into four categories: Methodology, Trends and Descriptive Futures, Alternatives and Reforms, and Journals-Bibliographies. It is well indexed and useful.

Annotated Bibliography on Educational Change. Center for Educational Reform (subdivision of the National Student Association), 2115 S Street N.W., Room 32, Washington, D.C. 20008. February, 1971. 22 pp.

Over a hundred items in the following categories: Radical Education Critique-Higher Education, Radical Education Critique, Educational Philosophy-Life Philosophy, Educational Psychology, Writings from the Classroom, Educational Publications, etc.

Rojas, Billy, *Future Studies Bibliography* (not annotated). Program for the Study of the Future in Education, School of Education, University of Massachusetts, Amherst. January 1970. 107 pp. mimeographed. 2,000 items.

Section XIII is on Education and the Future. It is broken down into General Trends in Education, New Educational Technology, New Curricula, Futuristic Aesthetics, and Futuristic Materials for and about Children.

Webster, Maureen, *Educational Planning and Policy: An International Bibliography.* Syracuse, N.Y.: Educational Policy Research Center (as above), June 1969. 654 pp.

Six major categories: Education and National Development; Comprehensive-Partial Planning; Financing Educational Plans; Influences on Plan Targets; Productivity and Efficiency; and Bibliographies. Organizes 4,900 items and is well indexed.

Confrontation: A Newsletter from the Lemberg Center for the Study of Violence. Special Issue on "Explanations of Student

Unrest." Weltham, Massachusetts: Brandeis University, April 1970. 23 pp.

Limited to colleges, but covers participants, issues, goals, processes, and outcomes. About seventy annotated items on student dissent.